focused living
in a frazzled world

105 snapshots of life

By Deborah P. Brunt

TATE PUBLISHING & *Enterprises*

TATE PUBLISHING
& Enterprises

Focused Living in a Frazzled World
Copyright © 2005 by Deborah P. Brunt. All rights reserved.

Book design copyright © 2006 by Tate Publishing, LLC. All rights reserved.
Cover design by Sommer Buss
Interior design by Lynly Taylor

Published in the United States of America

ISBN: 1-9332909-2-7
06.1.08

Dedicated to
the Lord Jesus Christ,
who gets a lot of bad press
but who alone gives perfect focus
to any frazzled life

Acknowledgements

Words cannot adequately express my thanks to:

My husband and hero, Jerry, and our daughters, Megan and Amanda, for your constant expressions of love to me and for continually allowing me to capture snapshots of your lives in print.

Everyone whose escapades found their way into this book. God has used each of you to show me things I otherwise wouldn't have seen.

Mindy Greve and Pam Whitley, for your invaluable help in preparing the manuscript.

The wonderful folks at Tate Publishing, for believing in me and working zealously to transform the manuscript into the published work you hold.

Table of Contents

Foreword

At a meeting of Oklahoma women to whom I had been invited to speak, I met Deborah Brunt. That first encounter was brief. Two pairs of brown eyes met and we greeted each other and exchanged contact information. In the year that followed, I remembered those brown eyes from time to time, little knowing that Deborah would soon become an important mentor to me.

We were to meet again in retreat settings in Oklahoma and a home setting in Texas. I soon discovered her deep commitment to women and passion for leading them into an ever-deepening relationship with Jesus Christ. I learned too that she wrote a regular column and asked if she would send me a copy each week. She kindly complied and with each reading I found myself unfailingly challenged, built up, and encouraged to persevere.

And now I have the privilege of making a heartfelt recommendation of Deborah's book, *Focused Living in a Frazzled World,* with its 105 very sharp, clear, colorful and untouched snapshots of life.

I found myself in each snapshot. Deborah identifies with me and therefore I with her, yet she never preaches at me. Being a rather serious type, laughing out loud is not something I normally do when reading, yet I find myself doing just that as she describes various impossible plights in which she finds herself. At other times I grieve with her, but never without hope. Deborah teaches me some very practical lessons too, such as the best of birthday gifts a person can give a friend in snapshot 52, and how to honor loved ones. The tribute in snapshot 100 can be adapted for personal use in many ways.

This book helps me with a deep personal need—that of proper focus—and I believe it will help you too.

As you read, I think you will be impressed by the writer's storytelling gifts. All the signs of a good narrative writer are there: for example, the setting of the stage on which the main characters meet, the introduction of the theme, and the employment of the five senses. We see the colors, hear the gun shot, feel the breeze and smell the honeysuckle. But the most important part of each snapshot is the drawing of the conclusion. As a storyteller myself, I always find that part the most challenging and difficult to attain. How should a story end? What is going to be the true conclusion that will leave all readers somehow changed for the better and wanting more? I think it is in the conclusion of each snapshot that Deborah's God-given gift shines through the most clearly.

This reader has certainly been left with a profound longing for more. How best to describe that longing? The writer herself says it best in snapshot 68. It is a " . . . deep, unrelenting thirst for God."

Pam Rosewell Moore
Waxahachie, Texas
April 2005

Introduction

Granddaddy always took pictures at family events. Trouble is, Granddaddy had one of those complicated cameras, where you have to get all the settings just right—*and* make sure the flash is working. What's more, Granddaddy didn't see well.

Every holiday, at the moment Grandmama placed the last steaming dish on the table and we all sat with forks poised, Granddaddy decided to capture the moment on film. While he fiddled with the camera and we tried to smile indefinitely, the feast grew cold.

Ultimately, he did snap several pictures—but I'm not sure how many of them were in focus.

In 1990, I started taking my own photos. Never able to conquer cameras and disinclined to insist that life pose unnaturally, I began writing weekly articles. The topics? Whatever appeared in my personal viewfinder as I paused to consider the week.

Over time, I began to realize how these mental snapshots had benefited me week after week. I also began to recognize the value for all of us of capturing a moment in time, holding it up to the light and contemplating it long enough to bring some aspect of life into perspective.

In our frazzled world, life is often a blur. We hurtle along, constantly changing directions, frantically looking toward all the places we think we should be, rather than really seeing where we are.

Losing our focus, we miss the very things that will take us where we need to go.

Jesus' closest followers weren't in nearly the hurry that we are, yet they often missed what they desperately needed to see. For example, these followers had front-row seats when Jesus fed thousands of people with five loaves and two fish *and* when he fed thousands more with seven loaves and a few fish.

Shortly after the seven-loaf lunch, the 12 headed out in a boat with Jesus. Mid-sea, the followers realized they had one loaf of bread for 13 hungry men. Was this a problem for Jesus? You do the math.

Hearing his followers' whispers, Jesus asked, "Why are you so worried about having no food? Won't you ever learn or understand? Are your hearts too hard to take it in? You have eyes—can't you see?" (Mark 8:17–18 NLT).

13

For 15 years, God has been teaching me to see what I'm seeing. When I started these weekly articles, our two daughters were preschoolers. As this book goes to press, the younger is preparing to graduate from high school, and the older is planning a wedding.

We lived five of these years in my hometown in northeast Mississippi, four in east central Indiana and the last six in Oklahoma City. As you peek at 105 selected snapshots from these three seasons in my life, pause and take a closer look. Wherever you live, you may find yourself in the frame.

You'll also notice that a story or verse from the Bible is mentioned in just about every snapshot. That's because the Bible's words are like a light shining in a dark place. Without that light, we're much like those 12 followers of Jesus: We have eyes but cannot see.

Please don't be put off by the references that tell where in the Bible you can find the quoted words—or by the abbreviations telling what version of the Bible I quoted from. The references are there in case you want to open up a Bible and check out the words for yourself.

So now, find a comfortable chair and look with me at some snapshots. Page by page, may God use these pictures to help you see what *you're* seeing—and to teach you focused living in a frazzled world.

Snapshot 1

□

Frapp Flop

Directions for drinking a bottled Starbucks vanilla frappuccino: Remove plastic wrapper from around bottle top. Shake drink slightly. Open lid. Drink.

Directions for disaster: Accidentally rearrange directions for drinking a bottled Starbucks vanilla frappuccino.

I hadn't yet left the house when it hit me: I was supposed to receive an overseas call on my office phone in 15 minutes. Sticking a frappuccino in my purse, I ran for the car. Then, remembering my agenda for the day, I ran back to grab three outfits, still in the bags from their respective stores. We were preparing to videotape several teaching sessions, and my orders were to bring the outfits to make sure they would "work" on camera.

To my great relief, I arrived at the office before the call came through. Hanging the still-bagged clothes on the hook inside my door, I booted up my computer. Next, I reached for the frappuccino, removed the plastic wrapper and opened the top.

My computer requested a password, so I set the frappuccino down and responded. Still focused on the computer, I reached for the bottle—and shook.

Vanilla frappuccino sprayed everywhere, soaking my pants and shoes, splattering across my desk and pooling on the plastic carpet-guard under my chair.

After an appropriate moment of silence, I called, "Janell! Could you bring a roll of paper towels?"

My assistant appeared in the doorway between her office and mine. For roughly a second-and-a-half, she tried not to laugh. While wiping up the mess, we decided on an appropriate plan of action: I would hide out in the women's restroom while she rinsed my pants, wrung them and handed them back to me.

Shoes sloshing, I headed for the ladies' room first. "No one told me washing your clothes was in my job description," she called after me.

When Janell opened the restroom door, I stood with one foot in the sink, attempting to rinse coffee from my pants leg. She asked, "What about—

"Those other outfits?" I finished. She nodded. "Would you see if one of the skirts will work with this shirt?" I asked.

Several minutes later, she reappeared without a skirt. "Your call came through," she said.

I dripped my way back to my office and closed both doors. Eager to get out of my now doubly drenched pants, I pulled a skirt from its hanger and slipped it on. The skirt didn't match, but my friend from overseas awaited.

After taking the call, I removed the tag from the blouse that matched the skirt I now wore. I was throwing the tag into the wastebasket before changing into the blouse when my new boss entered my office through my secretary's door.

There I stood, in a purple paisley skirt and an untucked brick-red shirt. Dripping pants draped conspicuously across a chair. Shopping bags hung in full view on the other door.

"Good morning!" I said brightly. We had an amazingly focused conversation, considering.

As soon as he left, one of my co-workers burned her pizza while laughing over my fiasco. Meanwhile, I headed for the restroom, still determined to change blouses and rinse my stained pants. Unbelievably, a sign now posted on the ladies' room door said: "Out of Order."

Alas. I'd gotten the frappuccino directions out of order—and now so was everything else. As I walked the hallways of our building, carrying bedraggled pants and searching for an available sink in which to rinse them, I was laughing too. At the same time, I was seriously praying something akin to *The Message* version of Psalm 40:17: *"And me? I'm a mess . . . make something of me. You can do it; you've got what it takes—but God, don't put it off."*

Snapshot 2

□

A Funny
Little Mama

"Tell us a Funny Little Mama story."

Our two dripping, preschool girls step out of the bathtub and make the same request at almost the same time. It's a familiar request, now.

Somehow, drying-off-after-bath-time has evolved into "tell-me-a -story" time at our house. And the most popular selections on our story list are homespun tales of the Funny Little Mama.

Let me clarify that last sentence a bit. The Funny Little Mama stories are the *girls'* favorites. Sometimes, they're not mine.

The girls like them because the Funny Little Mama is capable of just about anything. In one tale, she likes green beans so much she eats them at every meal (she even eats green beans on ice cream for dessert). In another story, she doesn't like green beans at all—until she finds out you're sup-posed to cook them before you eat them. One day, she's so tired she keeps falling asleep in the silliest of places and positions. Yet another day, she visits the three bears' house and cleans it while they're away.

The Funny Little Mama has a little girl who usually has to set her straight. The daughter teaches her mama what the bathtub is for (the Funny Little Mama thinks it's a very uncomfortable bed), how to take a bath (with soap and water, not just soap), and even how to take care of a baby (we're not sure how the little girl made it through babyhood).

I like the Funny Little Mama stories, too—after I've told them. But I often groan inside when the girls ask for one. Why? Because my daughters usually don't like their tales reheated. They want a new one every night.

By the girls' bath time each evening, my overworked brain is more than ready to idle a bit. Making up a new story, an interesting story, on the spur of the moment means kicking my tired mind back into gear. It means exerting a bit of energy that I often just don't feel I have.

Occasionally, I tell the girls, "I'm too tired tonight." But usually I relent and tell them their story. The thing that carries me past the "I can't tonight" barrier is this thought: Each extra effort I make to create for them a silly tale says to them, "I love you with God's kind of love."

As my daughters giggle, they're glimpsing a love that doesn't clutch or demand. Rather, it gives. It's built, not on feelings, but on choosing to act in another's behalf. One Bible writer expressed godly love when he told his friends, *"I will most gladly spend and be spent for you"* (2 Cor. 12:15 HCSB).

Amazingly, this spending doesn't leave us *depleted.* Rather, it makes us *completed.*

Unfortunately, God's kind of love isn't natural to any of us. As a matter of fact, it's impossible for us. Yet when we receive the God who is love, he miraculously reproduces his "love-ability" in us. He enables even a funny little mama like me to love in ways inside-out to what comes naturally.

◻

Ride the Roller Coaster— Without Losing Your Lunch

Life's a mess. One minute you're up, the wind on your face. You've been voted most likely to succeed. In cap and gown, you receive the diploma. You get the job, the promotion, the raise. You master that skill that's been eluding you. The love of your life slips the ring on your finger. The baby's a girl—and you can tell by the cry that she's fine. The person you least expected is giving you a compliment. You're laughing with a friend. You're cuddling a child. You're singing as you work. All's well with the world.

The next minute, you're down. You can still feel the wind, but now it hits against you, cold, biting. The drop has come so suddenly you feel you're going to lose your lunch. You flunked. You're laid off. The other candidate got the job, the promotion, the raise. Your fiancé wants to break the engagement. Your spouse wants a divorce. Your baby's sick. Your teenager is hurling stinging words to your face. Your "friends" hurl stinging words behind your back.

Your car breaks down. Your washing machine breaks down. Your life breaks down. You're tired. You're sick. You're angry. You're depressed.

Then, you're up again. The loan comes through. A new relationship buds. An encouraging letter or phone call arrives.

Life's a mess. One minute you're going one direction. You have a plan. You have a dream. You're sure the plan will get you to the dream. The next minute you're jerked around 180 degrees. Without warning, you find yourself barreling at top speed away from what you hoped to accomplish, where you planned to be.

You're still single, though you intended to be married by now. You're single again. You can't get pregnant. Your baby changes your life in ways you hadn't imagined. You leave the workplace. You enter the workplace. You switch careers. You relocate. Your youngest starts school. Your youngest leaves the nest. Now 20-something, your youngest moves back in. You become caregiver for an aging relative.

Just about the time you get oriented to each new course, your life takes off in yet another new direction. Up, then down, then jerked around, you're frightened and more than a bit queasy. Like a roller coaster rider at a fair, you hear yourself screaming...

Long before you and I were born, an Old Testament poet rode life's roller coaster. He surely faced as many ups and downs and hairpin turns as we. Yet he was able to say, *"I have calmed and quieted my soul" (Psalm 131:2 NKJV).*

Think of that! Hurtling downhill, he didn't yell. Yanked a different way, he didn't panic. Inwardly, he stayed on an even keel regardless which way he was thrown.

How did he do it? Ratcheting upward, he cried, *"Hope in the Lord" (Psalm 131:3 NKJV).* Plummeting downward, he cried, *"Hope in God" (Psalm 42:5 NKJV).*

To that ancient poet, *hope* involved looking toward and resting in. It wasn't a frantic grasping, but a sure grip, because the poet's hope was exceptionally well-placed. Confident, expectant, he handled life's bumpy ride by clinging to him who is always stable and ever able to *"make the rough places smooth" (Isa. 45:2 NASU).*

Life's a mess. It's sure to jerk you around. But the God of that Old Testament singer remains supremely in control. So when your stomach goes out from under you and you feel a scream coming on, cry to him. Hope in him.

Then, no matter how tumultuous the ride, you'll find to your great amazement that you can relax in his arms.

Snapshot 4

□

Jesus, Help Me!

Two-year-old Megan stood in the middle of a wading pool, her chubby knees slightly bent, her hands slapping the surface of the water. I sat at the poolside, my legs stretched into the pool, watching my daughter.

Behind me, older, rowdier kids splashed in a big pool. Nearby, other moms sat or lay in lounge chairs, catching a few rays and keeping an eye on their brood.

Without warning, Megan rose from her contented water-slapping position and, standing tall in mid-pool, cried, "Jesus, help me! Jesus, help me!"

Startled, I was ready to rescue her. But then, she calmly resumed slapping the water. Seeing she wasn't in distress, I sat wondering, "Did she say what I thought she said?"

The other mothers within earshot seemed not to have heard it. Or at least, they pretended not to notice. No one looked Megan's way. No one smiled. No one appreciated the moment—but me. I appreciated, even as I pondered: "What in the world brought that on?"

It wasn't until later that I realized where my toddler had gotten her cry. I was reading to Megan from her favorite Bible story book. One story told of 10 lepers, men whose bodies were so sick they couldn't go home to be with their boys and girls. The 10 heard that Jesus was coming. As he approached, they shouted: "Jesus, help us! Jesus, help us!" In answer, Jesus healed all 10.

Reading the story, I heard myself crying out almost the same words my daughter had yelled at the pool. There in the water, she'd apparently decided that, if sick men could cry to Jesus in front of a crowd, so could she.

Twelve years later, I sat reading a book titled *Not a Glimmer of Hope,* written by a new friend named Pam Whitley. Pam had a 21-year-old daughter, Jan, who had suffered profound brain damage eight days after birth. For more than 20 years, Pam had lived in an almost constant state of crisis as Jan grew, but remained a newborn—requiring round-the-clock care, suffering countless physical setbacks, and almost dying time and again.

Near the end of the book, Pam tells of the time when yet another bad report from Jan's doctor plunged Pam into the deepest depression of her life. She says, "It was as if I had fallen into deep waters, and I could not swim. I could see the *glimmer of light* at the surface of the waters, but I could not get to it."

Awake night after night with her hurting, crying child, Pam cried too and repeatedly prayed the only prayer that came to her numb mind: "Help me, Jesus. Help me, Jesus."

Help came in a most unusual way. A friend named Ginger who knew of Pam's struggle—but not her depression—had asked God, "Please let me help carry Pam's burden." Suddenly, for no apparent reason, Ginger found herself awaking with a deep sense of depression and the cry on her lips, "Help me, Jesus! Help me, Jesus!"

One day when Pam and Ginger talked, both realized what Pam verbalized: "Not only are you somehow experiencing what I'm feeling, but you are even praying what I am praying."

Pam says the realization that God had sent someone to share her load was one of the "life ropes that brought me to the surface out of the drowning depths of despair" (Spirit Press, 1993, pp. 151–154).

All of us have needs. Whether we're standing in shallow water or sinking in the deep, may we never be ashamed to cry out. Like Pam and Megan and 10 lepers of long ago, may we remember whose name to call. Whether others ignore us or pick up the cry, Jesus will help us.

Snapshot 5

□

Faith Has
a Pulse

The year was—oh, it could have been any year. All eyes were fixed onstage, where the action moved swiftly toward its climax.

In a highly dramatic, deeply moving, little-theater production of the melodrama, *Egad, the Woman in White,* by Tim Kelly, the two villains, Sir Percival Glyde and Countess Fosco, fought wildly. Beaten, the Countess died, slumping into a chair.

When sickly Frederick Fairlee suddenly appeared onstage, Sir Percival tried to cover the fact that the Countess was dead by pretending to be styling her hair. When Frederick fell asleep, Sir Percival fled. Then (drum roll), the hero and two heroines arrived.

Seeing the slouched body of the Countess, the three crossed to her. The hero cried, "You have much explaining to do, Madame." The two heroines (who were not as wise as they were beautiful) discussed the Countess' appearance:

"How strange she looks."

"And still."

"But rather lovely."

"I wonder who does her hair?"

Ultimately, the characters realized the Countess had no pulse and, therefore, was dead.

The audience laughed at the idiocy of characters who couldn't tell a living person from a dead body. I didn't dare laugh. I was busy being the body.

The year was—oh, it could have been any year. People were living lives that moved (more swiftly than they knew) toward the climax.

Many had found something they thought was faith. They freely admitted, "I believe in God."

The words sounded rather lovely. But as *The Message* version of James 2 asks, *"Does merely talking about faith indicate that a person really has it?" (v. 14).*

Living faith has a pulse. It moves. It breathes. Yet it is no actor, disguising pretense as reality. Rather, it's a *"seamless unity of believing and doing" (v. 25)* that grows out of utter yieldedness to the one and only God.

James 2:26 is rather blunt about the whole thing: *"The very moment you separate body and spirit, you end up with a corpse. Separate faith and works and you get the same thing: a corpse."*

In melodramas, dead bodies stand up and take curtain calls. In life, dead faith never budges. But just lying there, it fools a lot of people. That's because most folks like the sound of the word *faith*. It seems so lofty. It conjures up images of light and life. It holds such promise that good will come.

People will applaud a faith that calls attention to itself in some highly dramatic, deeply moving way. But few want anything to do with a faith that requires something from them, that indeed demands their lives.

The year was—oh, it could have been any year. I sat knee-to-knee with a woman, drawing a picture of what we'd just read in the Bible about faith. A chasm lay between her and God. She'd seen that no one is clever enough or good enough to bridge that chasm.

She'd read that the only one who could bridge the gap (because he's holy) did it (because he's love). Dying and rising again, Jesus threw himself across the chasm.

I asked, "Suppose you saw a swinging bridge over a deep gorge. What kind of faith would get you to the other side? The kind that plants feet on the ground and says, 'I believe that bridge would hold me'—or the kind that steps out onto the bridge?"

Living, breathing faith doesn't just answer the question. It acts. If the bridge isn't trustworthy, the person of faith is sunk.

People with pretend faith are much like Sir Percival, creating lovely "styles" with something utterly lifeless. Sadly, their performance often receives rave reviews.

Snapshot 6

□

The Circus

"Everybody in my kindergarten class is going to the circus this after-noon—except me," said Megan during lunch. "Mama, can we go to the circus sometime?"

"Yes, honey, we can go to the circus sometime."

"I've never been to a circus," said Megan.

"I've never been to a circus either," said three-year-old Amanda.

"Neither have I."

"Mama!" Megan exclaimed, incredulous. "You've never been to a circus?"

No, I hadn't. And though I didn't offer the children any hope of going to this one, I wondered what to do. I knew they'd love it. But my husband and I had recently begun learning to live on a budget. After much prayer, we had allocated our income the way we believed the Lord wanted it, and we had committed not to spend more than we had budgeted in any given area, if we could possibly avoid it.

Now at nearly month's end only three months into our budgeting venture, we didn't have any money left in the "leisure and entertainment" envelope. What money we did have in our account was set aside for other things.

I called Jerry at work and we talked. We knew we could finagle the money around some way, but we had mapped out our budget and agreed to abide by it because we believed God wanted us financially responsible and financially free.

After we hung up, I prayed, "Lord, we want to do what you want. We believe you've guided us to this budget. We're going to follow it. If you want me to take the girls to the circus, will you please provide the way?"

That was at 1:30. The first performance started at 4:00. At 2:00, an acquaintance from church phoned. It was, in fact, the only time I can ever remember her calling me. She said, "Would you like two tickets to the circus?" (She and her husband had just been given two extras.)

I took her up on her offer, remembering that Amanda had some leftover birthday money I could use to pay her way in. Thinking a direct answer to prayer had never been quicker, I called, "Girls, guess what?"

As we stood in line at the ticket counter outside the big top, another acquaintance ran up. "Do you need a child's ticket?" she asked. "We have one too many."

"I know I'm going to cry now," I told the girls.

We walked inside the tent and found seats near the center ring. The show started. We thoroughly enjoyed the lion tamer, the acrobats, the tightrope walker, the horses, the elephants and the clowns. In fact, Megan, Amanda and I loved the whole two-hour performance.

But if anyone asks us the most memorable thing about our first circus, we'll have to say: "The tickets." (Thank you, Lord.)

Snapshot 7

❑

The Most Unwanted Assignment

Somewhere along the way, you've gotten an assignment you didn't want. Someone in authority handed it to you—and there you stood, wanting with everything in you to hand it back.

In that instant, you could: (a) refuse the assignment, (b) delegate it to someone else, (c) plead to be relieved of the assignment, or (d) do it reluctantly.

Okay, there *is* a fifth choice: Do the unwanted assignment cheerfully.

Ha!

In school, we learned tricks for getting around assignments. Many people have spent lifetimes perfecting this art. But though the teacher may believe we read the book when we really skimmed the *Cliffs Notes,* though the boss may think we created what we really found on the internet, it's a different story when God gives the assignment.

You can try to fool him, but I wouldn't recommend it.

Imagine you're a member of a prestigious family, a cousin to the President. You've held a minor political office, and people are throwing your name around in connection with a very sought-after position.

Suddenly, God gives you the following assignment: "Shout with the voice of a trumpet blast; tell my people of their sins!"

Your political counselors tell you, "Not a smart move." Your friends and family tell you, "Not a smart move." Your own brain tells you, "Not a smart move."

But way back in Old Testament days, when God told Isaiah that very thing, a man who might have enjoyed political stardom didn't ignore the assignment, hand it off, plead for God to give it to someone else, or use passive-aggressive behavior to let God know his displeasure.

Isaiah accepted the assignment. And he didn't do the bare minimum needed to get by. For 60 years, he shouted "with the voice of a trumpet." Tradition holds that he died when a king, who did not want his atrocities labeled as sin, had Isaiah sawn in half.

One weekend I was driving from Ft. Worth to Oklahoma City and stopped for gas about midway. I'd been using the drive time to pray. Stepping back into my car, frappuccino in hand, I was still thinking about God. Out of nowhere, this Scripture reference came to my mind: Isaiah 58:1.

Curious to see what it said, I pulled my Bible out of my briefcase and looked it up. The words leapt up, throttling me: *"Shout with the voice of a trumpet blast; tell my people of their sins!" (TLB).*

As I sat in my car at the gas station, tears trickled down my face. Not this assignment!

Only a week earlier, I had stood before a group of Christians reading a Bible passage in which God confronts his people with their sins. I made no comments—just read. In response, one woman wrote, "You can't open a rose with a sledge hammer."

So maybe God isn't trying to open roses. In Jeremiah 23:29, he asks, *"Does not my word burn like fire? . . . Is it not like a mighty hammer that smashes rock to pieces?" (NLT).*

God knows we like warm and fuzzy, chocolate and flowers. He offers everyone of us a deeply intimate love relationship. Ah, but his love stuns us. When he sees rock-hard hearts running toward disaster, he throws down the bouquet and trumpets the truth.

Usually, he uses people's voices. Inevitably, some hear the shout and turn back, but others, refusing to stop or turn, lash out at the trumpeters.

Exposing sin may well be *the* most unwanted assignment. Still, the God of relentless love seeks people who will accept it. Sometimes, he finds them at gas stations.

Snapshot 8

□

Cowgirl

Long before we ever lived in Oklahoma, our younger daughter Amanda decided she wanted to be a cowgirl. Where she got the idea, I do not know. But one day when she was three, she rummaged in our closets until she found a hat that looked enough like a cowgirl hat to suit her, and she wore it everywhere.

That afternoon, while we were out running errands, she decided she also needed a cowgirl outfit. As she plotted aloud what it would be—jeans skirt, red shirt, boots—I wondered where she'd gotten such accurate knowledge. If she had lived in the early days of TV, she'd have seen it in all the westerns. But long before her formative years, the westerns had ridden off into the sunset.

"Mama," she asked, interrupting my reverie, "Would you help me learn to stay up on a cow?"

Sputtering, I tried to explain to her that cowgirls didn't ride cows; they rode horses and roped cows. At first, she did not believe me. But when we got home, she let her older sister make her a stick horse and a hair-ribbon lasso.

The next day, dressed in the outfit she had assembled, she told her daddy, "What I really need is a real horse."

"Oh, you do?" he answered. Then he asked, "Where did you learn so much about cowgirls, anyway?"

Amanda replied, "I just thought about it . . . and from Mama's Bible."

Jerry asked her for chapter and verse.

If you'll watch a test-your-knowledge TV game show when one of the categories is "Bible," you'll see that our daughter isn't the only one who has ever made off-the-wall comments about what the Bible says. People who can answer the most trivial of questions about other topics don't have the foggiest idea about the simplest Bible facts.

Pop quiz for all who care to take it:

• Who asked, "Am I my brother's keeper?"
• Who preached the Sermon on the Mount?
• Tell three of the Ten Commandments.
• Name three of Jesus' disciples.

Recently, I sat beside a woman on an airplane who told me, "I know Jesus died on the cross for our sins, but I don't believe that he's the only way to God. He never claimed to be."

I showed her Jesus' words in John 14:6: *"I am the way and the truth and the life. No one comes to the Father except through me."*

She said, "I can't accept that."

"Well, you don't have to accept it," I told her, "but as you can see, he did say it."

Even those of us who attend church regularly may, in the same breath, say things that are amazingly correct and appallingly confused. That's because we might like to know what the Bible says, but we're not exerting ourselves to find out.

Yet, 2 Timothy 3:16–17 tells us, *"The whole Bible was given to us by inspiration from God and is useful to teach us what is true and to make us realize what is wrong in our lives; it straightens us out and helps us do what is right. It is God's way of making us well prepared at every point, fully equipped to do good to everyone"* (TLB).

You see, the Bible holds, not only the answers to the pop quiz above, but also the answers to life. Trying to live life without consulting it is like trying to be a cowgirl without boots, hat, lasso, and horse. It's like trying to ride off into the sunset on a cow.

Snapshot 9

□

Ethan's Song

He has cancer of the throat. Two years ago, she had a brain hemorrhage. She almost died. He's lost 30 pounds (though he didn't have 30 pounds to lose). Unable to eat, he drinks liquid supplements to keep going, but he's extremely exhausted, sometimes unable to function.

He tries to be strong for her. She tries to be strong for him, but the stress brings on the horrible head pain associated with her brain hemorrhage.

Unbelievably, the two of them continue to put together an annual writers' conference each summer. In the midst of their own struggle, they've refused to sit down, to focus inward. Both writers themselves, they're still trying to help others who want to learn better how to capture life in words.

I've been thinking about the two of them a lot lately. Today, I've also thought about a writer named Ethan. Mostly, I've been pondering a song Ethan wrote.

To catch you up on everything that's known about Ethan: He was a wise man and a singer who lived thousands of years ago. So here's what brought Ethan to my attention: He wrote one song that still hasn't gone out of print. Originally written in Hebrew, it's been translated into English and hundreds of other languages. You probably have a copy in your home. It's named "Psalm 89." (I read it in *The Message* version.)

Like my two friends, Ethan believed in the God he called "Father," "God of the Angel Armies" and "Rock of Salvation." Ethan set out to sing a song to this God.

As songs go, it's rather long. It's also rather wonderful, because it takes us where we least expect it to go. *"Your love, God, is my song, and I'll sing it!"* Ethan begins. *"I'm forever telling everyone how faithful you are."*

For nearly three-fourths of his song, Ethan continues saying good things about God. In particular, he keeps pointing out God's love and faith-

31

fulness: *"Your love has always been our lives' foundation, your fidelity has been the roof over our world,"* Ethan declares.

Then, without warning, Ethan makes a dramatic turn: *"But God, you did walk off and leave us." "You tore up the promise you made to your servant." "How long do we put up with this, God? Are you gone for good?" "Where is the love you're so famous for, Lord? What happened to your promise?"*

Some people today would applaud that final stanza—but lop off everything that goes before it. Looking at life, they've decided God doesn't exist or, if he does, he isn't a God of faithfulness and love.

Others of us, wanting poetry that inspires, would feel much more comfortable if Ethan's poem ended in the middle. At the very least, we'd rearrange the song, putting the last stanza earlier, so that the crisis goes hand-in-hand with a happy-ever-after ending.

Yet, Ethan didn't quit writing when his thoughts about God contained more questions than answers. Nor did he throw away his words of faith on expressing thoughts that seemed to contradict them. Instead, standing in the midst of crisis, Ethan wrote the whole song.

What's more, when God heard Ethan's song, he didn't feel threatened. He didn't get angry. He didn't scold. He said, "Put that song in my Book. A lot more people will want to sing it."

My two friends are probably singing Ethan's song about now. They still believe in a God who is faithful, a God who is love. But they must sometimes wonder where He's gone.

And that's okay.

Snapshot 10

□

Shopping for Hearts

God is shopping for hearts. From my slot on the last rack, I see him enter the store. I eavesdrop as he approaches the store owner. "Not fancy hearts of paper and lace," he says. "Hearts of flesh."

"Oh, I don't know," the owner answers. "I don't have many of those."

God indicates he wants to look, anyway.

First, he peruses the racks marked "Unbelievers," "Atheists," "Agnostics," and "Nice People Just Trying to Get By." There, all sorts of hearts beat inside every type person you can imagine. But the owner is right. Only a few children's hearts, and the hearts of one or two adults who've never heard God's truth, are still flesh. The rest show various stages of calcification.

God strides toward the "Christian" racks, including the small one at the back where I have a slot. As he examines the hearts around me, I can tell he's appalled. Most of the hearts on these racks are stony too.

Shaking his head, he murmurs, "I told them. I specifically told them not to imitate unbelieving hearts."

Then he scolds all of us who bear the label *Christian*. From my perch on the little rack, I try to avoid his eyes. "Do you see how hardened you've become?" he asks. "In your case, as in theirs" (he motions to the unbeliever hearts), "the hardening has taken place gradually over a period of time. But for you, it's worse.

"All around you, voices are clamoring: 'Truth is relative. We each have our own truth. You alone can decide yours.' Yet, I am truth, and you are able to hear my voice. Daily, I've told you the truth. Each time you've received what I say—hearing accurately, doing accordingly—you've become softer and more pliable. But every time you've rejected truth or tried to create your own, you've calcified a bit more."

In spite of myself, I meet his gaze. Instantly, I recall a truth I recently read in Isaiah 30:15—*"In repentance and rest is your salvation, in quietness and trust is your strength, but you would have none of it" (NIV)*.

I've wanted rest and quietness, but—well, okay: I've had none of it. I've fretted instead of trusting. I've made excuses instead of repenting. I've listened to the voices telling me, "That verse sounds poetic and sweet, but it just doesn't jive with life. Frankly, honey, you're an anxious person. You've lived with anxiety a long time. You might as well make your peace with it."

But today, under God's stare, I see the real reason I haven't conquered anxiety. "You hardened your heart," God says quietly. Then, he crosses to where the store owner waits.

"I'll take them all," he announces.

"All those hearts of stone?" the owner asks. "I thought you wanted hearts of flesh."

"I do." Turning to address all of us, God repeats what he said ages ago in Ezekiel 36:26. His voice resonates through the store. *"I will give you a new heart and put a new spirit in you; I will remove from you your heart of stone and give you a heart of flesh" (NIV)*.

He pauses. Then, measuring his words, he tells the owner, "I'm going to give everything I have to pay for them all. But I'll only take the ones who agree to come—the hearts willing to hear and follow my voice, to feel what my heart feels."

He lays open his wallet.

"Take me!" I cry.

Snapshot 11

□

Blink

I always have tears in my eyes. So do you. God placed tiny holes behind our eyelids to produce the tears. And then he created a way to spread those cleansing tears across our eyes. It's called *blinking*.

You've probably not thought a lot about blinking. You'll never see a TV feature story on "people who blink." And even in casual conversation, no one will likely ask, "So are you blinking a lot these days?"

Blinking is just something you do, without any fanfare.

On those rare occasions when you do hear about blinking, the context will probably be negative. For example, a photographer will warn, "Don't blink." Or, as you drive past a tiny, rural community, someone will remark, "If you blink, you'll miss it." Or you'll find yourself muttering about a person whose excessive blinking drives you crazy.

But don't undersell the blink. For all its bad (or nonexistent) press, blinking is vital. Imagine talking to a person who never blinked. The unbroken eye-to-eye contact would leave you uneasy, unable to think, and totally undone within a few minutes.

Imagine having to make a conscious effort to blink. If God hadn't put blinking under "automatic functions" in your body makeup, you would have to tell yourself every few seconds, "It's time to blink. Blink. Okay, blink again." You'd rarely have time to think of anything else.

Or worse yet, imagine that you couldn't blink at all. It happens, you know. Lori, a high school senior, suffered a severe head injury in a cheerleading accident. Subsequent surgery left the right side of her face paralyzed. Until another surgery corrected the problem, Lori had to hand-blink her right eye and to tape it shut when she went out in the weather.

I read about another young woman named Katie who underwent brain surgery twice as a result of a brain tumor. Five years later, Katie's left eye still wouldn't blink. She had to keep salve in it, which meant she couldn't see out of it.

During a troubled time, the writer of Psalm 77 cried out to God, *"You have held my eyelids open" (v. 4 NASU)*. I think I understand how the psalmist felt. One Saturday night, my paternal grandfather died rather suddenly. After the call that woke me with the news, I lay on my back in bed, staring into the night, unblinking.

I'd lost my two living grandparents and an aunt in less than four months. Yet, the tears that are always in my eyes seemed to evaporate. Because I couldn't cry, I had no release.

The next time you see a picture of yourself smiling at the camera—with eyes closed—don't groan. Instead, frame the picture. Keep it as a reminder that the God of infinite detail enables you to blink.

Snapshot 12

◻

Cricket Encounter of the Loudest Kind

So there I was, sound asleep in a conference center lodge room when a cricket decided to serenade me. He started his song so suddenly, so loudly, I sat straight up in bed.

The sound was raucous, insistent, unnerving. Fumbling for the light switch, I donned my flip-flops and flip-flopped across the room. Careful search indicated my latter-day Romeo was singing to me from just outside my door.

Afraid to open the door for fear he'd jump right on in, I did what any self-possessed person would do at 3:30 in the morning: I kicked the door. The cricket stopped chirping. I tumbled back into bed, turned off the light and was dozing again when the racket erupted a second time.

Pulling myself out of bed again, I kicked the outside door *and* turned on the bathroom fan. When the little guy got over the door kick, even the roar of the fan couldn't drown his shrill song.

The third time I got up, I decided that, eventually, kicking the door was going to wake the neighbors. Emboldened by desperation, I threw open the door, raised a flip-flop and prepared to strike. Sure enough, there he was, Romeo the cricket, sitting in the crevice where the door swings open.

I hit at him with the flip-flop. He jumped. I hit. He jumped. Out across the concrete sidewalk I chased him—me in my gown, he in his glory. Finally, confident that I had chased the critter away, I clambered back into bed and fell asleep.

Romeo tuned up again exactly 15 minutes later. I couldn't believe it. He'd hopped back to the same cleft in my doorway and was chirping his little heart out.

Once again, I chased him with a flip-flop. Once again, he gave me the slip. Once again, I fell into bed, confident I'd sent his strident song elsewhere. When the chirping erupted anew, one inspired thought leapt to mind: "Hair spray!"

Flip-flopping to the bathroom, I grabbed my weapon. Flip-flopping to the door, I flung it wide, took aim and sprayed.

I sprayed Romeo. He hopped away. I sprayed the crevice he loved so well. All in all, I emptied about half a can of mega-hold onto the sidewalk just outside my door.

Then, almost afraid to hope, I slipped back into bed.

Silence. Ahhh.

Chir-r-r-r-r-rp! Oh no! My last, best weapon had failed. I was defeated.

But this time, the song that began with gusto ended like a music box running down. Mega-hold took the vibrato out of Romeo's legs. My adversary had won a lot of battles, but he had lost the war.

I have another adversary who poses as a suitor, who attacks when I least expect it and who appears unstoppable. He's a master of slick maneuvers and can unerringly find the one spot most likely to undo me.

Unlike Romeo, this adversary messes up my life on purpose. Because he can't be seen, many say he doesn't exist. That gives him an even deadlier edge.

But though he's won innumerable battles, he too has lost the war. Hebrews 2:14 tells me God's Son became human and died in order to *"render powerless him who had the power of death, that is, the devil" (NASU).*

Thanks to Jesus, the world's most abrasive and lethal song will one day grind to a halt. Even now, my best weapon is his mega-hold.

Snapshot 13

□

Exposed

I used to think I was a pretty good person. Not overly selfish. Fairly patient. Reasonably even-tempered.

Then I had children. And they continually expose me.

My precious little preschoolers ask for one more thing from the refrigerator when I've just sat down to the table for the fourth time. They plant their feet in cement when I say, "Hurry!" They pull out everything in the toy closet, promising all the while, "We'll put it back." Then they throw a fit when I insist they do what they've promised.

So how do I respond to all these thoughtless deeds? I act impatient and angry and selfish. Of course, it's all their fault. In fact, I sometimes think that if my children were perfect, I'd have no trouble being perfect myself.

But then God reminds me that if the selfishness were not already there, hidden somewhere down deep inside, I would have no trouble getting back up from the table for the fifth time. And if patience were built into me, I could deal firmly, but gently, with foot-dragging. And if I were truly slow to anger, I would not get angry so quickly when my children beg to be excused from their household jobs.

The truth is, I've had these wrong tendencies all along, but B.C. (before children) my ugly attitudes had less opportunity to rear their heads, and so I foolishly thought I'd conquered them. Now, those closest to me have a way of yanking the lid off what I think I've gotten rid of but have really only buried.

So what do I do when my ugly attitudes are showing? Sometimes I try to whitewash my wrongdoing or put the blame on those who exposed me. Sometimes I decide to change the subject. Sometimes I attempt to provoke pity by crying and threatening to turn in my mother's license.

But all those reactions bury the wrongs deeper, where they can grow

39

and fester. Freedom and healing come only when I say to myself, to God, and to my children, "I was wrong. Will you forgive me?"

I've learned from experience the truth of Proverbs 28:13: *"He who conceals his sins does not prosper, but whoever confesses and renounces them finds mercy" (NIV)*.

Some of the sweetest times in my family life have come when I confessed to my children what they already knew but needed to hear me say: "I blew it." Then I let them know, "I'm going to keep on trying to cooperate with God to replace ungodly attitudes with godly ones."

I used to think I was a pretty good person. Now, I know the truth. But I don't despair, because my children not only expose me, they also encourage me.

Once, when I had humbled myself to confess a wrong, Megan smiled, patted my hand and said, "You do have a problem with your temper, Mama. But you're doing better."

Snapshot 14

■

Wherever You Are

The setting looked quite ordinary. Rows of folding chairs filled a large activity room. The chairs faced a small stage. Those of us with purple t-shirts and khaki pants were preparing to present a program. As the women arrived, I shook hands with a number of them, exchanging names and brief pleasantries. On many faces, I met broad smiles. In many eyes, I found an unmistakable light.

Three were very pregnant. One of them announced that her baby was overdue. We invited her to sit where she could exit quickly. Another young lady entered the room showing pictures of her newborn.

While we visited, a purple-shirted man set up equipment, checked mikes, then began playing lively CD music over the sound system. The ladies responded immediately to the music, standing, clapping, swaying. Someone spontaneously led out and, soon, a growing line of women clapped, swayed and danced its way around the perimeter of the room.

At time to start the program, the women gave a standing ovation to the man who welcomed them. He introduced a comedian who barreled into the room from the rear, hurling down the center aisle decked in pompadour wig and outlandish clothing. Uproarious laughter erupted—and didn't stop till he left the stage. Either he was the funniest man I've heard in a long time, or we were all just set for a loud, long laugh.

"My face muscles hurt, I laughed so much," one lady said afterward.

After the comedian came a singer—an Oklahoma man who had sung for many years with the gospel group, the Imperials. Then, a woman spoke and, finally, a cowboy from Texas serenaded us with country-western tunes.

Every one of those artists was four-star. And yet, I'm telling you, they were not the main attraction. The audience was. The energy in that crowd was electric—but never out-of-hand. Every time a song started, women stood to move to the music. We clapped in time until my hands hurt. Laughter flowed freely, and so did appreciative comments called out at appropriate times to those on stage.

When the singers talked between songs, the women listened. But when the lady speaker had her say, the hush in the room was palpable. The energy didn't dissipate. It just held its breath. The lady was telling her story. The women strained to hear it.

You see, her story was their story—at least in part. She had been where they are. Everything in them identified with the hopelessness she'd felt. Everything in them cried for the hope she offered.

Yes, the room looked quite ordinary. But outside, floodlights shone down on a tall fence topped by rolling barbed wire. The shirts each woman wore said "INMATE" in large block letters across the back. We were meeting in a maximum security prison.

The lady who spoke had been in and out of prisons and mental institutions, eaten up with liver disease from drug and alcohol use, rejected and abandoned by birth parents, adoptive parents, and anyone else with whom she'd tried to live. Now she's married, rearing her children, active in church.

She assured the women that Psalm 146:7 is true: *"The Lord sets prisoners free"* (NIV). She explained how God's one and only Son Jesus does that. She insisted, with John 8:36, *"If the Son sets you free, you will be free indeed"* (NIV). Many nodded vigorously as she spoke.

After the program, the women filed back to their cells. Walking out past guards and gates and barbed-wire fence, I knew: Wherever you are, you can be imprisoned. Wherever you are, you can be free.

Snapshot 15

□

Cashews and Other Deadly Poisons

Holiday parties, wedding receptions, and baby showers often have something in common: mixed nuts. And party guests passing a container of mixed nuts often do something alike: They pick out the cashews and eat them first.

If you're a nut lover wanting to save a few cents, you can probably find bags of unshelled pecans, walnuts, and peanuts on your grocer's shelf. But you won't find unshelled cashews there.

Until roasted, cashews are not edible. In fact, the unprocessed nuts contain a caustic oil so poisonous the US government bans the import of unshelled cashews.

For you to enjoy these tropical nuts, someone somewhere must go to an inordinate amount of trouble.

Several years ago, I read that in Malawi, east Africa, cashews are first boiled in oil to extract most of the poisonous oil. Then, factory workers pry open the moon-shaped nuts with fingernails or hand-operated nut-cracking machines.

Next, other workers scrape the nuts by hand, one at a time. At that time, a typical worker might turn in 11 pounds of scraped cashews a day, earning about $1.

Yes, unprocessed cashews are full of deadly poison. You certainly don't want to pop one into your mouth. But just in case you haven't read the warning: Something already in your mouth is also *"full of deadly poison."* James 3:8 (NIV) identifies this something as your tongue.

Because James wrote a long time ago, you may want to believe he was writing about someone else. Surely, he had your spouse, your teen, your coworker or your neighbor in mind when he placed his "Warning! Poison!" label on the tongue.

But, remember, cashews in the shell look innocent, too. And like people's tongues, every one of them is deadly.

More bad news: You can never process the poison out of your own tongue. David—a sheepherder, songwriter and king—tried. Here's how he described the experience in *The Message* version of Psalm 39: *"I'm determined to watch steps and tongue so they won't land me in trouble. I decided to hold my tongue as long as Wicked is in the room. 'Mum's the word,' I said, and kept quiet.*

"But the longer I kept silence the worse it got—my insides got hotter and hotter. My thoughts boiled over; I spilled my guts" (vv. 1–3).

Why couldn't David detoxify his tongue? For the same reason you and I can't. In Jesus' words recorded in Matthew 15:18, *"The things that come out of the mouth come from the heart" (NIV).*

Whenever poison spews from your tongue, poison is hiding in your heart. You cannot rid yourself of that hidden poison; it's too deeply buried. But someone else has gone to an inordinate amount of trouble to create a clean heart for you. The process extended from his birth through a 33-year lifespan and death by hanging on a cross which (get this) he did in your behalf.

So the next time you grab a handful of mixed nuts, consider what it takes for an African factory worker to transform a deadly cashew, and remember: Only the one who gave his life for you—and lived to tell about it—can miraculously transform your tongue.

Snapshot 16

□

Somebody's Keeper

At the ripe age of six, Megan was her sister's keeper. At least, that's the impression I got when I listened to a conversation she and four-year-old Amanda didn't know I overheard.

The two were in the tub. They were supposed to be soaping, rinsing, and getting out. Instead, they were playing Soap Monsters, a game whose purpose and rules they alone knew. Just across the hall from the closed bathroom door, I stood in the laundry room sorting clothes and trying to decide how long I was going to let the game go on before getting them back on track.

Without warning, Megan interrupted their play, crying out with authority, "Stop!"

"I don't have to obey you," Amanda retorted.

"Yes, you do. I'm your elder sister," Megan asserted.

Amanda snickered over the phrase "elder sister." Megan declared, "It means 'older sister.' And what if you were about to get hurt and I yelled 'Stop!' Wouldn't you obey me?"

"If I was about to get hurt, I'd just stop and not get hurt," Amanda said.

"Well, I told you to stop playing Soap Monsters because Mama said to finish bathing; and if we don't, we're going to be in real trouble."

"And we'll miss supper," Amanda added.

The two got on with the task of bathing. No one missed supper. Later, when bedtime rolled around, the family congregated on Amanda's bed. Megan opened our *Early Reader's Bible* to the story of Onesimus.

The slave of a Christian named Philemon, Onesimus stole some items and ran away. Hundreds of miles down the road, Onesimus met a man named Paul and became a Christian himself. Paul urged Onesimus to go back to Philemon and make things right. Paul also wrote a letter urg-

45

ing Philemon to accept Onesimus back—not as a slave, but as a Christian brother.

How opposite the actions of Cain, that ancient older brother who killed his sibling out of envy! When asked by God, *"Where is your brother Abel?"* Cain replied, *"Am I my brother's keeper?" (Gen. 4:9 NIV).*

Paul, by contrast, neither harmed those close to him nor refused to get involved when they were harming themselves. Rather, he wrote, *"I appeal to you on the basis of love" (Philemon 9).* Paul risked hearing, "Mind your own business!" to encourage two brothers in Christ to make right (but hard) choices.

At the end of the story about Paul, Philemon and Onesimus, Megan read the questions in the *Early Reader's Bible* that family members would take turns answering. The last question asked, "How can you help others do what they should?"

I knew how one elder sister could have answered. But I was almost afraid to consider the question myself. In a culture that values independence so highly, it's a delicate thing to be somebody's keeper—even (and perhaps especially) if the person is a close friend or relative. Yet, before God we too have a responsibility to make appeals on the basis of love.

The Soap Monsters episode happened years ago, but today I still find myself asking: When someone close to me is making wrong choices, am I willing to try to help that one avoid disaster, even at the risk of receiving only snickers or comments to the effect, "I don't have to obey you"?

When the occasion demands, do I care enough to cry, "Stop!"

Snapshot 17

☐

Make This Problem Go Away

People all around me are hurting. Fran is grieving over a rebellious teen. Alice is trying to get on with life now that her husband of 30 years has married another woman. Joanne and her family are battling constant illnesses. Marlene is struggling with a difficult pregnancy.

And me? Well, I'm just having trouble sleeping. It's not that my mind is weighed down with worry (though that does happen occasionally). I have a physical condition called mitral valve prolapse that is somehow connected to a glitch in my autonomic nervous system.

Often, when my body's supposed to be on idle (as in the middle of the night), my insides rev up for no reason. I wake up and can't get back to sleep. Over time, this can become a rather exhausting practice.

I have a favorite prayer I pray those nights I find myself hopelessly awake. It is: "Please help me go back to sleep."

People all around me are probably praying something very similar. No, they're not necessarily asking to go to sleep. But they are asking, "Please, make this problem go away."

I don't know how much headway they're making, but many nights, God has ignored my request. At times, I've accused him of being hard of hearing or worse, hardhearted. When you're really sleepy or really stressed or really sick or really hurt, it's easy to accuse God of a lot of things.

But if I've learned anything during my nocturnal vigils, it's that jabbing God with angry words in hopes of provoking some response, simply doesn't work.

James, a New Testament writer, suggested why God often refuses to budge when we ask for relief from a difficult situation. He said, *"You know that under pressure, your faith-life is forced into the open and shows its*

47

true colors. So don't try to get out of anything prematurely. Let it do its work so you become mature and well-developed, not deficient in any way" (James 1:3–4 MSG).

James also suggested a rather different prayer to pray during hard times. *"If any of you lacks wisdom,"* James began (gently suggesting that we all do lack wisdom), *"he should ask God, who gives generously to all without finding fault, and it will be given to him" (James 1:5 NIV).*

In the midst of troubles, escape may sound like the best option. If God doesn't engineer it, most of us are tempted to do so ourselves. But forced escape puts us in the same position as a felon on the loose. Even though we may have found a way to "bust out" of the immediate problem, we're not free. With the hounds of our own immaturities at our heels, we're constantly in danger of finding ourselves right back in the place we tried so hard to flee.

It's wisdom that helps us keep on keeping on, holding us to the right path until we get through to the other side. It's wisdom that ensures the trial accomplishes God's purpose—not of destroying us—but of perfecting us. It's wisdom that, ultimately, brings release.

So now, my new favorite middle-of-the-night prayer has become, "Please give me wisdom. And please give Fran wisdom. And please give Alice and Joanne and Marlene wisdom." It's amazing how many people you can pray for when you're not wasting time lashing out at the one who's trying to help you grow up.

Snapshot 18

□

Dining with Dignity

If you're planning a really nice social gathering, you may want to invite me to sit at the head table. This will provide just the right touch of comic relief.

Just make sure you're prepared for comic relief.

One insightful person recently invited me to an upscale luncheon. After finding the downtown building where the luncheon was held, I parked, entered the building and stepped into an elevator with four other women. They were discussing an upcoming trip to Paris that one of them was taking.

Sensing that they were not overjoyed to have a stranger intrude on their space, I tried to make myself as inconspicuous as possible. Not an easy feat in an elevator.

Shortly, we stepped out into an elegant dining room with a stunning view. I tried to look as if I always dine in such places, but standing at the window with mouth agape, I felt like Gomer Pyle on *The Andy Griffith Show*. Gomer would encounter something new and delightful by yelling, "Golly, Andy! Go-o-olly!"

I was told to sit at table # 11. Arriving at table # 11, I was told, "No. Someone had to cancel. Would you please move up to the head table?"

Except for a previous two-second meeting with the hostess of this shindig, I knew no one. What someone canceling had to do with my moving to the head table, I still don't know. But I obediently picked up my purse and walked.

Uh-oh. The round table to which I'd been pointed had eight seats. Four were empty. In the other four sat the ladies from the elevator. I chose a seat and tried to make conversation. Didn't go well. I picked up the program and read the bio of the guest speaker. Several things in the bio intrigued me.

Soon, the speaker and her friend joined us. Excited to have someone to talk to, I began asking questions based on the information I'd just read. With very little trouble at all, I managed to offend the speaker twice—first, by asking about an honor she hadn't received and, then, by showing my ignorance of her position.

The four, who had chatted among themselves until I began talking to the guest speaker, were now watching with great interest while I tried to eat both feet.

Lunch was served just as our hostess joined us. After cutting bite #3 of the chicken and gravy (and shortly after my second verbal faux pas), I was laying down my knife and changing hands with my fork (as we lefties have to do). But instead of picking up the fork, I launched it, catapulting onto my lap the bite of meat and gravy I was just about to eat. Thankfully, most of the mess went into my napkin.

Though everyone at the table saw the fowl fly, no one cracked a smile. Only my hostess acknowledged that the incident had occurred. "Those things happen," she whispered.

Perhaps the others were trying to protect my feelings. Perhaps they were trying to preserve decorum. Frankly, I'd have felt better if everyone had laughed uproariously at my expense. I think the other ladies would have felt better too. Elegant luncheons and stunning views are wonderful, but taking oneself too seriously can cause indigestion anywhere. And, as the wise writer of Proverbs said, *"A cheerful heart has a continual feast"* (Proverb 15:15 NASU).

Having deftly displayed my inability to dine with dignity, I saved my laughter for the return elevator (which I rode alone) and the car. In laughter, though, I felt a bit sad. I missed the bond eight women could have shared if we had quit putting on airs and enjoyed the moment together.

Snapshot 19

□

Ant Lessons

"Okay, Okay, that's it. I'm setting the timer." I had asked Megan and Amanda to fold the mound of towels and socks that had adorned our den chair for two days. Towel-and-sock folding is one way the girls earn a little money each week.

After conferring, the two agreed that five-year-old Amanda would tackle the towels, while seven-year-old Megan sorted and stuffed socks. But while dividing the pile, the girls forgot the purpose of their mission and ended up in a game of laundry toss. When I peeked into the room, they were throwing towels from chair to chair and socks from chair to floor.

So I set the timer. They knew what that meant: If the job wasn't finished when the timer went off, they would still have to complete the work—but wouldn't get paid.

It would have been much easier for me to fold the clothes myself the day I set them on that chair. But I've told the girls, "In this family, every member contributes." And I'm trying to live out that principle.

The two are well aware of the simple duties they're required to accomplish each week—some for pay, some not. Yet, when I must keep reminding, set the timer, or withhold privileges because of jobs left undone, I'm tempted to think the day will never come when they tackle the towels and socks without coercion as soon as they see the piled chair.

And maybe it won't. Those playing by today's rules tell me I'm wasting my time even to try to teach my children to take initiative and be industrious. Assuming people are incapable of these qualities—and somehow abused if asked to develop them—many leaders now urge: "Ask not what you can do for your country (family, employer, etc.). Ask what everyone else can do for you."

But Proverbs 6:6–8 offers different advice: *"Take a lesson from the ants, you lazybones. Learn from their ways and be wise! Even though they have no prince, governor, or ruler to make them work, they labor hard all summer, gathering food for the winter" (NLT).*

Suppose we get past our irritation over being called "lazybones"—and take that advice. We find a tiny anthill and watch the goings on. What will we see? Busy ants, working in harmony—with purpose.

We won't see any ants loafing on the job because the boss isn't looking, or doing only what someone has forced them to do (and that not very well), or spending their whole work day planning the playtime afterward. We won't see worker ants paralyzed by backbiting, back-stabbing and competition among the ranks.

We won't see slick ants bargaining to get the most benefits for the least amount of work. We won't find able ants refusing to work, yet expecting to be fed.

We won't see teenage ants expecting adult privileges without the accompanying responsibilities. We won't find young adult ants still enjoying life at Mama's and Daddy's expense.

If ant brains can direct ant bodies in wise ways, surely people created in the image of God himself can learn to take initiative, be industrious and work in harmony to do what needs to be done—even if someone occasionally has to set the timer to remind us.

Snapshot 20

□

Jewels

If you ever want to give me a gift, I do accept jewels.

My grandmother on my mother's side loved jewelry, and Grand-daddy had the wherewithal in his later years to buy things for her: opals, emeralds, rubies, sapphires, diamonds. In retirement, they took numerous trips to the other side of the world. Each time, Grandmama would come back with a brooch or earrings or a necklace that dazzled us all.

This week, I took a trip to the east side of the Mississippi River—and found some dazzling jewels myself.

The place I went didn't have a mall, or even a jewelry store. It did have motel-type rooms and a lodge with various meeting rooms. It also had tall pines, rolling hills, and a small lake.

The room where we met for approximately 27 hours a day had no windows. All the better *not* to see the pines, hills, and lake, I suppose. Ah, but we did get a rather generous lunch break. And two of the days, I gulped down my food and headed outside to the lake.

The first day, the sun was out; the sky, practically cloudless. I ambled awhile along the lakeshore, then sat near the water's edge.

With tall pines bordering the lake on three sides, the winter sun had to reach a point rather high in the sky in order to shine directly on the water. It reached that point as I sat.

Without warning, a hundred diamonds danced on one section of the water. They were diamonds such as I'd never seen before—precise, many-faceted, brilliant, almost blinding. I sat, transfixed by the fact that they'd appeared so suddenly and dazzled so thoroughly. Finally, grinning with delight, I walked back to the room without windows, carrying a treasure-trove of diamonds in my mind.

The next day at lunch, I almost didn't walk down to the lake. A high overcast blocked the sun, and a damp cold penetrated my jacket. No dia-

53

monds today, I thought. Still, the pines and the water seemed preferable to sitting indoors, waiting for another session to start.

Reaching the water's edge, I walked round the lake in the opposite direction from the day before, ultimately finding a single wooden bench at the far side. Seated on the bench, I noticed how green the water looked—far greener than the previous day. Were evergreens above or algae below contributing to the color? I didn't know. But the richness and depth of the green captivated me.

Emerald. Where yesterday there were diamonds, today an expanse of emerald. And there on the emerald pallet emerged a shimmering picture of upside-down-trees and lowering sky—not appearing suddenly, but coming into focus gradually; not brilliant, but soothing. I sat, transfixed by the gentle beauty of the scene.

You'll be pleased to know I brought a lot of information back from the meeting. But, like my grandmother, I wanted to show you the jewels. And I want to publicly thank the one who gave them to me. After all, it's not every day that someone presents you with the biggest emerald you ever saw and a whole host of the most exquisite diamonds imaginable.

I'm confident who the giver is—even though he offered the jewels anonymously—because a wise man named James wrote in his New Testament letter: *"Every desirable and beneficial gift comes out of heaven. The gifts are rivers of light cascading down from the Father of Light" (James 1:17 MSG).*

Ah, yes, rivers of light cascading down from the Father of Light—creating treasure I can carry with me always.

Snapshot 21

◻

Entrails

If you're not eating, could we discuss entrails? The subject came up recently as I sat in a circle of women pondering—of all things—Leviticus.

Generally, women don't ponder Leviticus. But, hey, they go to R-rated movies. So these women blew the dust off a rarely read Old Testament book and found verse after verse of blood and guts.

Let me tell you, the sacrifices God required of the Jewish people were messy. Burnt offerings, peace offerings, sin offerings, guilt offerings—only the grain offering didn't involve a cut-up animal.

In each case, the sacrificed animal was a stand-in for the person who brought it. In each case, the body of the animal was handled according to instructions God specified in detail. According to Hebrews 9 in the New Testament, that's because every act of sacrifice gave a sneak preview of a better sacrifice to come. The New Testament even goes so far as to say that God himself became the one bloody sacrifice completing all the others.

So, meanwhile, there's this business of internal organs—inner parts, bowels, guts, if you will. Every time God goes to describing an animal offering, he talks about "entrails," as well as *"the fat that covers the entrails and all the fat that is on the entrails" (Lev. 3:3 NASU,* and *several* other verses). The inner parts had to be washed. The guts had to be handled just so in order for the offering to be pleasing to God.

Interesting, isn't it, that those animal parts represented people's hearts?

Want to know God's description of our human entrails? Warning: It's R-rated. You may be offended. But for those brave enough to look, Psalm 5:9 says, *"Their inward part is destruction itself" (NASU).* The Amplified version is even more graphic: *"Their heart is destruction [or a destructive chasm, a yawning gulf]."*

If that's not enough, God also says that basically, down deep, we're fools. No, I'm not kidding. Would I kid about a thing like that? Here's a direct quote (about us human types) from Psalm 49: *"Their inner thought is that their houses are forever and their dwelling places to all generations . . . This is the way of those who are foolish" (vv. 11,13 NASU).*

If all this is true, inwardly we're a mess. But here's the good news: God doesn't hate our guts. According to the Bible version of history, he created our guts. To start with, they were good guts. But early on, a deliberate act of disobedience changed all that.

David, one of the guys who took notes for God in the psalms, describes the universal human birth defect that resulted. In the same breath, David cries for God to do what's needed to change him inwardly:

"But I was born a sinner, yes, from the moment my mother conceived me. You deserve honesty from the heart; yes, utter sincerity and truthfulness . . . Don't keep looking at my sins—erase them from your sight. Create in me a new, clean heart, O God, filled with clean thoughts and right desires . . . You aren't interested in offerings burned before you on the altar. It is a broken spirit you want— remorse and penitence. A broken and a contrite heart, O God, you will not ignore" (Psalm 51:5–6, 9–10,16–17 TLB).

So here we are, discussing entrails. No, it's not a pretty word, nor a pretty subject. But when I move from discussing animals to exposing my own inner self to God's purging fire, the bad is burned up—and a new me emerges from the ashes.

Snapshot 22

□

Funny Thing

I was a serious child. Big brown eyes, long brown hair, I studied each situation before speaking. Today, people still think I'm frowning at them when, in reality, I'm *concentrating* on what they're saying.

My parents knew that a lighter side lurked inside me somewhere. From my earliest days, they cultivated it. In the afternoons of my childhood, Mama would hear me belly-laughing as I watched the Three Stooges' slapstick humor on TV. At night, when I fussed over the indignity of early bedtime, she'd pretend to run into the door facing on her way out of my bedroom. The more times she did it, the harder I laughed.

Warning: If you fall down in front of me, I'll be glad to help you up—but only after I regain my composure. Once, a friend named Laurie knocked over a rack of potato chips at a convenience store where we'd stopped en route to a concert. Just recalling the incident, I laughed again.

Ah, and who could forget the Camel Walk. Even in my teenage years (when nothing parents do is funny), Mama could make me laugh by doing a dance that, yes, looked like a camel walking.

Daddy took a different tack. He created humor with words. To him, the dictionary is just a suggestion for language use. Definitions, pronunciations, even the words themselves can be reinvented at will.

When I learned in science class that table salt is sodium chloride, chemical symbol NaCl, Daddy began asking us at meals to pass the "sodium nacl" (pronounced "nackle"). In the days before TV remotes were born, he would say to whichever of his offspring happened to be in the room, "I'm going to think of a number between one and 10 and the one who gets the closest can change the channels!" Inevitably one of us would say a number—it might be 5 or 225—to which Daddy would reply, "That's it! How did you guess?"

While Mama taught me to *see* humor, Daddy taught me to *hear* it.

But there were two things this serious child never encountered from my parents as I laughed my way through childhood. One was humor that belittled people. Daddy's word plays never contained sarcastic put-downs, and Mama's antics never mocked anyone. She imitated the Stooges, yes— but never made fun of people whose real-life actions we might have thought odd.

What's more, my parents never exposed us to raw humor. The laughter ladled out to me so generously contained no sexual innuendo, gutter meanings or irreverence. To use a term popular in my youth, it wasn't gross.

Many kids today don't know how to laugh without slamming someone or bringing up the verbal equivalent of vomit. They've grown up on a steady diet of vulgarity ingested from TV, movies, school and—all too often—home.

The Bible says, *"Obscene stories, foolish talk, and coarse jokes—these are not for you" (Eph. 5:4 NLT)*. Why? Because there are two kinds of laughter.

One kind warms our hearts as it fills our mouths. It's contagious— prompting laughter in those who hear. It heals and builds up, not only the one laughing but anyone in earshot.

The other kind is hollow, chilling hearts as it erupts from mouths. It prompts anger and tears—or, even worse, deep tiredness. It can be echoed but never caught. It hurts and tears down, not only those who listen, but also the one laughing.

Sad to say, now that I'm all grown up, I hear all around me the laughter of death. But as for me, I'm committed to doing what my parents did— passing on the laughter of life.

Snapshot 23

□

Trifles

Generally, I recognize a bowl. But this one was disguised.

It was given to me at a church gathering, wrapped in tissue paper tied with a gold ribbon. Removing the tissue, I saw what appeared to be a giant clear-glass handbell—without the ringer. The fluted handle of the "bell" was just right for grasping. Yet, staring, I couldn't quite grasp the purpose in such an object.

Seeing my puzzled expression, a woman across the table from me offered a helpful tip: "If you'll turn it over, I think you'll see that it's a trifle bowl."

Aha. What had appeared to be a rather cumbersome bell turned out to be a lovely bowl. Its "handle" was instead the base, like the stem of a crystal drinking glass.

The kind woman across the table explained that trifle bowls do indeed hold trifles, or whatever else you choose to put into them. Nodding sagely, I scurried home to consult my trusty dictionary.

Not only had I not recognized an upside-down trifle bowl when I saw one, I'd never heard of a trifle—at least not in reference to food. In my past encounters with the word, a trifle had always been something insignificant or unimportant. This definition, Webster affirmed. Yet, definition #2 described something entirely different: "a dessert of sponge cake spread with jam or jelly, sprinkled with crumbled macaroons, soaked in wine, and served with custard and whipped cream."

Marlena Spieler clued me in even further in her online article published in the *San Francisco Chronicle,* December 18, 2002.

Marlena identified *trifle* as a British dessert that dates back to Shakespearean times. In something akin to Elizabethan verse, she described the dish as, "sloppy, gloppy, sweet and frothy . . . like the perfect creation you dreamed of as a child." For those of us who might want to try a trifle but don't imbibe, she suggested substituting juice for the wine.

"A trifle is more about architecture than it is about culinary technique," she said. "You can 'build' your creation with ingredients to suit your passion." The ladies at the church had suggested angel food cake, vanilla pudding, custard and whipped topping.

"Even a really terrible cook . . . can make a delicious trifle," Marlena announced.

Now that's good news. But it's still disconcerting to discover there's a food that's been around since the 1500's, and I'm just now learning about it. It's even more disconcerting to receive a gift—and not know which end is up. Little comfort that I'm not the first person who's gotten things upside-down when it comes to trifles.

A lady named Martha wanted the meal to be perfect when Jesus came to visit. Her sister Mary wanted to hear everything Jesus said. Mary *"sat before the Master, hanging on every word."* When Martha interrupted them, angry because her sister wasn't helping in the kitchen, Jesus told Martha, *"Only one thing is essential, and Mary has chosen it"* (Luke 10:39,42 MSG).

On another occasion, he announced, *"You're hopeless, you religion scholars and Pharisees! Frauds! You keep meticulous account books, tithing on every nickel and dime you get, but on the meat of God's Law, things like fairness and compassion and commitment—the absolute basics!—you carelessly take it or leave it"* (Matt. 23:23 MSG).

Usually, I know a bowl when I see one. Usually, I know a trifle when I see one. But occasionally someone has to show me what should have been obvious, to teach me what I should have already known.

Thank God for folks who will say, as strongly as needed, "You're looking at things the wrong way."

Snapshot 24

□

The Same Sun

Our daughter Megan, then 8, appeared in our bedroom doorway. It was time to leave for school, but she wasn't ready to go. Barefoot and distraught, she had a fine-tooth comb lodged firmly in one side of her hair.

For some reason she just could not recall, she had decided to twirl the comb, rather than use it to straighten her part, as instructed. She'd done such a good job of twirling that I finally had to render the worst of all possible judgments: "We'll have to cut your hair."

Even with as careful cutting as possible, a mass of sandy brown hair went into the trash.

Megan cried over the lost locks. But she didn't get angry with me. Repentant, she said, "I'm sorry." Then, she and I worked together to fix her hair so the gap didn't show. Later, a trim at the beauty shop helped shape the short section until it could grow back.

In case you're wondering, this daughter never tried the twirling trick again.

In another time and place entirely, a political leader had a different tangle. In his country lived a host of people God wanted to free. But when the Lord told him, "Let my people go," the man just held on tighter.

To loosen this dictator's grip, God began a series of assaults: The country's water turned bloody and foul. Frogs covered the land, hopping into beds and kneading bowls. Biting gnats, then blood-sucking gadflies swarmed. An epidemic swept through the livestock, killing horses, donkeys, camels, cattle and sheep. Painful sores erupted on people and animals. Hail, then locusts, destroyed remaining crops and livestock, as well as any folks foolish enough to stay outside. Utter darkness and, finally, rampant death visited the land.

Before rendering each judgment, God gave fair warning what was coming—and opportunity to avoid it. Time and again, he repeated the simple solution: *Let go.* After each assault, God asked, in essence, "Can you hear me now?"

More than once, this leader said he would let go—but then didn't do it. Rather like certain modern-day leaders, Pharaoh of Egypt repeatedly hardened his heart—and so brought greater and harsher devastation on himself and his nation.

So what? So this: The same sun that melts the butter hardens the clay.

Both the girl and the leader felt the heat of the consequences of foolish actions. In that heat, the girl melted. The leader hardened. In each case, the response revealed the nature of the heart.

We live under the same sun as that long-ago Pharaoh and my eight-year-old daughter. Each of us has twirled the fine-tooth comb of resolve to do things "my way"—only to find we've made a tangled mess. We've all suffered loss as a result of choosing an inadvisable path.

But here's the question that reveals the state of our hearts: When we feel the heat, when God gives us fair warning that the course we're on is a destructive one, do we harden—or melt? Do we grow more determined to continue in the same direction? Or, repentant, do we say, "I was wrong," and then turn from our harmful behavior?

Proverbs 29:1 warns, *"A man who hardens his neck after much reproof will suddenly be broken beyond remedy" (NASU).* When we're tempted to think we can get away with a little neck-hardening now and then, we'd do well to remember—Pharaoh.

Snapshot 25

□

Sucker Holes

If you hang out with the airport crowd long enough, you'll pick up a term seasoned pilots use. I learned it from my husband shortly after we married. In those young and carefree days, I often traveled with him when he flew his company's twin-engine plane to call on customers across the eastern U.S.

One day we stood at a windswept airport (passenger alert: all airports are windswept). Surveying the sky as only pilots can, he said, "There's a sucker hole."

"A what?" I asked.

Whereupon I gained a valuable insight. In seasons of inclement weather, a large patch of blue sky will sometimes appear. Thinking the sky has cleared, beginning pilots may venture out, only to find themselves surrounded by clouds.

Even in those days, my husband was an experienced pilot with instrument rating. Clouds did not daunt him. He'd been trained to use the instruments and flight plans that would keep him flying right-side-up in the right direction, regardless whether he could see anything beyond the airplane window.

Beginning pilots should not fly through clouds, but not of course because the clouds are sharp or hard. You might think the greatest danger that pilots face when flying in clouds is getting lost or running smack into something they can't see. Those are dangers. But the greatest danger lies in suddenly not knowing what's up and down and right and left. That's due to spatial disorientation that happens when a person in flight cannot see a visual reference outside the plane.

Pilots can encounter tragedy by being drawn into a sucker hole.

But novice airplane pilots aren't the only ones who've mistaken a sucker hole for open sky. Long ago, a ship lay docked at a small port on the island Crete. The ship's crew wanted to sail 40 miles to another, better harbor. The weather had been terrible for sailing, but the sky cleared and a moderate south wind came up. Both the pilot and the captain decided conditions were favorable for the short voyage.

Nobody listened to a prisoner aboard ship named Paul. Paul was not an expert in nautical weather. Nor did he have clout. Yet, Paul had a direct line to the one who directs the weather. And Paul warned (Brunt paraphrase), "Men, we're headed into a sucker hole."

Sure enough, a violent storm sprang up just after the ship left harbor. Strong winds carried the vessel hundreds of miles off course. Before the crisis ended, crew and passengers had ditched every bit of cargo, lost the ship, and nearly starved. If not for Paul's presence, everyone on board would have died.

Today's pilots have a luxury the captain of Paul's ship did not. Before setting out, they can call a reputable weather service to find out whether the sky has truly cleared or is luring them into disaster.

Most of us will not set out today aboard a small plane or sailing vessel. Yet we *are* on a journey. And all too often, we're easily deceived by what appears to be true. So, hey, let's learn to emulate wise pilots.

Yes, there's a reputable service we can call—and we don't even have to pick up the phone. In fact, you can't reach this service by dialing an 800 number. *"Call to me and I will answer you,"* says God himself. *"I'll tell you marvelous and wondrous things that you could never figure out on your own"* *(Jer. 33:3 MSG)*.

The one way to avoid life's sucker holes? Call on the one who knows where you're headed—and heed the wondrous advice given.

Snapshot 26

□

Mind Games

Does your mind mind? Mine doesn't. In fact, you could say my mind has a mind of its own. My thoughts are stubborn little devils running insistently down forbidden paths while my better instincts cry, "No! Don't go there!"

Of course, the farther my mind runs, the fainter my protesting voice becomes. And the fainter my protests, the more sure my thoughts are that they can take me where they will.

In particular, my errant thoughts love to frolic on Anxiety Avenue. This is a broad street, with lots of fret stops (similar to bus stops, only you get on for the ride and it takes you nowhere).

It makes no difference whether I'm trying to sleep or to focus on a task at hand, whether life is humming along or stalled, whether there's a reasonable cause for concern or not. My mind can get to Anxiety Avenue from any point at any time. Just between you and me, I think my thoughts like to take anxious paths because they get a kick out of seeing panic grip my heart.

This mind of mine scurries to worry about: what I have done—and what I haven't. What I should (or shouldn't) have said. What my family members have done, are doing, or might do. What the newscasts report. What the weather forecast means. What might happen. What others think.

Indeed, the possibilities are limitless. Whatever the topic, my mind can find an anxiety angle. It especially likes to catch me napping. That is, those moments when I'm hovering between sleep and waking are the moments I most often find myself gripped by thoughts of woe. In my half-conscious state, all of life appears fraught with peril:

"You forgot to . . ."

"What if . . . ?"

"Oh, no!"

Now understand, I'm not telling you this so you can feel sorry for me. I'm telling you this because I suspect that you also may struggle with wayward thoughts. Maybe, like me, you tend to worry. Or maybe worry isn't your problem. Maybe your mind runs to bitterness or envy, criticism or complaint, craving, resentment, despair or any of a host of negative places.

Whatever the specifics, many of us find that our thoughts like to frolic in mind-fields. Down deep, we know this isn't good. Yet, all too often we stand wringing our hands over the bully within our own brains.

Here's where we do well to remember: Bullies aren't necessarily stronger. In fact, they're mostly bluff. Regardless of what may seem true, undisciplined minds can be tamed. Our thoughts don't have to rule us. In fact, our thoughts should not rule us. We should rule them. I know this because a man named Paul said so. And he had it on good authority from God himself.

In Philippians 4, Paul wrote to us worriers: *"Do not be anxious about anything, but in everything, by prayer and petition, with thanksgiving, present your requests to God. And the peace of God, which transcends all understanding, will guard your hearts and your minds in Christ Jesus"* (vv. 6–7 NIV).

Then, Paul addressed all of us, instructing, *"Whatever is true, whatever is noble, whatever is right, whatever is pure, whatever is lovely, whatever is admirable—if anything is excellent or praiseworthy—think about such things"* (v. 8 NIV).

My mind doesn't like to mind. But if I let it roam where it will, my life will be miserable. If, however, I grab firm hold of my wandering thoughts and relentlessly present them to God, the one who made my mind will teach me to tame it.

Snapshot 27

☐

Fools Trust Floaties

"Think deep thoughts," the speaker challenged us.

"We'd rather go to the dentist," you could almost hear the audience reply.

When it comes to thinking, we're baby-pool waders. We eye the few who head for the diving board, and shake our heads. The deep end looks too difficult—too time-consuming. Not nearly as inviting as the shallow.

So, most of us decide to spend our lives mentally crammed into the baby pool. There, we may sit or splash or sun. But we do not swim. We cannot swim. There's not enough water. Who wants to swim, anyway?

Problem is: Thinking is not a summer sport. It's a vital life skill. The wise writer of Proverbs said, *"For as he thinks within himself, so he is" (23:7 NASU).* If we think shallow, we are shallow. And though our minds may stay in the baby pool, our lives will not. The situations we face are deep and treacherous, and the choices we make will drown us.

Not wanting to drown, we've resorted to—floaties. Instead of trying to think for ourselves, we latch onto the thoughts of others, hoping desperately that they'll buoy us up. It doesn't matter that others' reasonings may be as ill-thought-through as our own. It doesn't matter that the thoughts to which we cling may have been so often regurgitated—rather like forwarded e-mail—that they make no sense whatever. We like our ideas preprocessed, pre-packaged, pre-cooked.

Two recent experiences have made me realize how prone to shallow thinking I am. First, I read *How Now Shall We Live?* by Charles Colson and Nancy Pearcey. It took weeks to finish the book, partly because I have little reading time, partly because the book is long and partly because I'm so unused to thinking deeply that I had to reread whole sections.

"This material is so compelling," I thought. "We desperately need to know it. But will we make the effort?"

Then, I attended a conference in New Mexico. One of the workshop leaders walked to the front of the class—and dove immediately into the deep end. All through that first afternoon, he urged us to follow. There were places I couldn't keep up with him, but the effort was invigorating. And what I did see impacted me more deeply than anything else at the conference.

That evening at supper, an acquaintance asked me, "What did you think of that workshop?" I could tell by the way she asked the question she had no intention of venturing out of the wading pool.

Deep thoughts require time. In our hectic world, we say we don't have time to ponder, but we do. We can turn off the radio when we're alone in the car—and think. We can turn off the TV, find a quiet spot—and think.

Deep thoughts require work. Our mental muscles have grown flabby from lack of use, but they don't have to stay that way. We can welcome the challenge of the thought-provoking, rather than shying away from it.

Oh, and one more thing: Deep thoughts require God. I know that's a controversial statement, but it didn't originate with me. The Proverbs writer said, *"The fear of the Lord is the beginning of knowledge."* The God who created all things is the source of every on-target thought on any subject. Bow before him and you're on your way to understanding more than you can begin to conceive.

Not interested? The Proverbs writer completes his thought this way: *"Fools despise wisdom and instruction"* (1:7 NASU). In a world of high tides and crashing waves, fools trust floaties rather than learning to swim.

Snapshot 28

□

Is God
Pro-choice?

If there's a God, he's pro-choice.

I know this because daily life requires so many choices: what clothes to wear, what food to eat, what brand to get, what channel to watch, what shoe to put on first, what task to do next, what response to make when hurt or belittled or questioned or encouraged, what thoughts to think, what emotions to show, what words to say, what relationships to build, what job to accept, what purchases to make, what details to handle, what ways to handle them.

Each day's choices range from the mundane (whitening toothpaste or tarter control?) to the life-changing (relocate or stay?). A quick trip to the store can overwhelm us with the sheer magnitude of the choices before us.

My mother once walked into the grocery to find the new husband of my best friend standing helplessly in front of the milk cooler. "Beth said to get milk," Richard told Mama. Beth hadn't prepared him for the array of choices he'd face—size, brand, fat content. Those were the days before cell phones, so he couldn't stand in the aisle and call home for directions. Mama chose for him, sticking a gallon of whatever she deemed appropriate into his buggy.

Being both postmodern and smug, we might not see choice as having anything to do with God. After all, we're the ones doing the choosing. But if there is a God, surely he could cancel all options, forcing us to conform as a dictator does his subjects. Since we have choices—and plenty of them—anyone up there running the universe must be in favor of it.

What's more, we might not see choices as having anything to do with right or wrong, wise or foolish. We may boldly state that any choice is right for me as long as I choose it. If the results are less than desirable, we can always wave around the word *victim*. Everyone understands this to mean that other people (and even society as a whole) may make wrong choices—even though I may not—and it is their wrong choices from which I am suffering.

Too, we can always help each other sidestep the consequences of our—er, unfortunate—choices. A car lot offering creative credit, for example, boasts a large sign announcing, "Bankrupt? No problem."

Meanwhile, the God of the Bible has his own large signs in place. They announce that the universe runs by certain rules we cannot change. We make "wrong" or "foolish" choices when we crash into those rules, expecting them to bend just for us. We make "wise" and "right" choices when we stay within the spacious boundaries these rules provide—much like a child who plays happily in a wooded playground next to a busy interstate, rather than trying to climb the fence.

One other thing: Not only does God not have to give us choices, he doesn't have to tell us which ones will hurt us and which ones will help. Yet the Bible is chock full of specifics designed to steer us toward wise choices in every area of life.

This God, who claims never to change either his character or his standards, says in Deuteronomy 30:19, *"This day I call heaven and earth as witnesses against you that I have set before you life and death, blessings and curses. Now choose life, so that you and your children may live" (NASU).*

Interesting, huh? The God who offers choices wants us to make the right ones and teaches us what they are. That's because, if there's a God, he's pro-life.

□

Surviving the Lucy Syndrome

I'm an adult. I should be able to handle a mild culture change—say from Mississippi to Indiana—with no problem. But alas, within weeks of moving away from the Deep South with my family, I had contracted the Lucy Syndrome.

This syndrome—which I myself discovered but humbly chose to name after another—is so called in honor of—no, not the gal who always frustrated Charlie Brown, but rather the gal who always frustrated Desi.

The symptoms first appeared one August afternoon when my daughters and I went to pick up the mail. Emerging from the Yorktown post office with several letters, we scurried to the car and waited our turn to pull out of the parking lot onto the busy highway that runs through the center of town.

Finding an opening at last, I made a right turn into the traffic. The next instant, I saw an odd sight in my rearview mirror. It was our mail, fluttering onto the highway behind us. Vaguely, I remembered setting the stack of letters on top of the car while helping the girls get buckled in.

Moaning, I pulled into the parking lot of a nearby bank, jumped out of the car and stood at the edge of the highway. For the next several minutes, my daughters and all passersby watched as I would (a) find a break between unslowing cars with grinning drivers, (b) run into the street and retrieve an item of mail, (c) turn and dash back to the curb, and (d) repeat the procedure until I had picked up each piece of our tire-tracked letters.

To my chagrin, this was not a passing malady. Ever since, I've continued to recreate my own *Lucy Show* episodes.

One week, for example, I flew to Denver. In that impressive new airport, my bags and I joined a long, slow-moving line at the car rental desk.

When I finally reached the desk, the lady there told me, "We're a little short on cars right now. We should have you one in about 30 minutes."

I had just bought myself a cup of praline frozen yogurt and sat down to wait when the same lady looked straight at me and called, "BURNT!" She had found me a car earlier than expected.

Clutching yogurt, purse and car rental agreement, while at the same time pulling a wheeled carry-on with folded hang-up bag perched atop it, I ran toward a shuttle that was almost full. The driver closed the doors in my face, then reluctantly opened them again.

When I tried to step up into the shuttle, the carry-on overturned, spilling the hang-up bag. I couldn't retrieve either because of the other 97 items I was holding. Sighing, the driver came to my rescue, while a bus full of men in business suits pondered the question, "Why did this idiot lady buy yogurt when she's already got too much to carry?"

As we drove in silence to the car lot, I downed the yogurt quickly, hoping to avoid a repeat performance when time came to exit the shuttle. On the lot, the driver stopped at car after car to let people off. When I alone was left, he told me, "Uh, the car you're supposed to have isn't here."

With a grin, I replied, "I'm not surprised this happened to me."

Somewhere along the way, I'd read the prescription for my ailment found in Proverbs 17:22. It says: *"A cheerful heart is a good medicine" (NIV).* It means: To survive the Lucy Syndrome, you have to learn to laugh at yourself.

Snapshot 30

□

Invitation from God

What would you do if God invited you to visit?

Let's suppose this wasn't your first meeting with God. No. You first met him when a natural occurrence took a decidedly supernatural turn. You stopped to look. God spoke up, enlisting you for a task much bigger than you could handle. Terrified at first, you soon found yourself asking questions.

To your amazement, God answered. He gave you details, assurances, even abilities you knew were beyond you. You kept trying to bring the conversation back to your inadequacy, but he just kept announcing who he is and what he planned to do.

Suppose the task God gave you involved leadership. In considering this task, you saw a few minor obstacles: (1) The people you were supposed to lead already had a leader who did not intend to step down. (2) The people themselves didn't want you to lead them. (3) You'd tried to lead these folks previously and had messed up royally.

In spite of yourself, you began doing what God said. You delivered messages to people who didn't want to hear them. You took actions that at first appeared ludicrous, then became dangerous. This didn't make you popular. You chose not to use manipulation, coercion or force, yet God so transformed the situation that you emerged the leader.

Now you have a wad of people to guide—and we're not talking about a Sunday School class here. More like a mob. Yes, they're supposed to be God's people, but the kindest term God can find to describe them is "stiff-necked."

From day one, they have complaints and conflicts—so many that, even after you delegate much of the decision-making, your time is more than filled just trying to referee.

Knowing you need God, you've prepared a convenient spot to meet with him. But he begins calling you to meet him on a mountaintop. This is not an easily accessible mountaintop. You have to do some serious climbing to get there. He calls you once, twice, three times, four times.

Just when you're ready to say, "Lord, remember that little place we used to meet just a block from my office," he calls a fifth time, saying, "Come up to Me on the mountain and be there . . ."

Could you see yourself saying, "Look, I'm too busy. Let's compare calendars. Maybe we can pencil something in for, say, an afternoon next summer."

All of the above really happened to a man named Moses—except that Moses never told God he was too busy. In the throes of trying to lead some 2,000,000 people, he climbed a mountain seven times to meet with God. One of those times, God didn't say a word for six days. Two visits lasted 40 days each.

All in all, Moses threw away nearly three months that he could have been making decisions, handling problems, checking off items on his to-do-list. But during his time with God, he learned everything he needed to know to lead wisely. He learned everything the people needed to know to live well.

What would you do if God invited you to visit? Would you acknowledge his existence? Would you recognize his voice? Would you deem his invitation a lovely idea—but impossible to work into your schedule? Would you cancel everything else to come?

Romans 1:21 in *The Message* version says, *"People knew God perfectly well, but when they didn't treat him like God, . . . they trivialized themselves into silliness and confusion so that there was neither sense nor direction left in their lives."*

Moses didn't make that mistake. Will we?

Snapshot 31

□

Snoveralls

Yes, Virginia, there is snow in Indiana. But we were beginning to wonder for a while.

It was August when my family and I moved north. At the grocery, the gas station, the churches we visited, and the tire store where I stopped to ask directions, people noticed my accent and asked, "Where are you from?" When I drawled, "Mississippi," they would warn, "Well, just wait till winter."

I heeded their warnings. In September, we all got heavy coats. In early October, we purchased gloves and snow boots. Then we waited. And waited.

We finally got snow on December 9. It set a record—for being the latest first snow of the season in central Indiana. For my girls and me, it set a different record. It was the first ground-covering snow we had seen in seven years. At that time, Megan was two, and Amanda was an infant.

Now nine and seven, the girls were ready to have some serious fun. Over heavy clothes, they donned coats, gloves, and boots. Tramping across the street to the yard of a friend named Janna, they romped and squealed and built their first snowman.

When the three finally came inside to get hot chocolate, I found out we weren't as fully prepared for the snow as I had thought. My girls' gloves were soaking wet, as were their pants. Their fingers, hands and legs felt icy cold. "Janna says we need snow gloves," they informed me, "and snowsuits."

I had to ask Janna's mother Rose where to shop for snowsuits. Locating the suggested store, I found one rack of what looked like black padded overalls made of nylon with polyester filling. I wouldn't have known they were snowsuits, except that Janna had worn something similar the day she and my girls built the snowman. I bought the suits, as well as two pairs of insulated gloves. Then we waited. And waited.

Finally, just in time for New Year's, it came: another real snow. Donning heavy clothes, "snoveralls," coats, boots, and new gloves, the girls headed outside again. When they came in for hot chocolate several hours later, their cheeks were rosy, but all their body parts were dry and even semi-warm.

In late February, our girls had not yet tired of playing in the snow. One day after school, they donned their snoveralls and ran out to build a snow fort on our back deck with several children from the neighborhood. Watching them through the sliding glass door, hearing their laughter and knowing their gear was indeed protecting them from the cold, I realized how much better I am prepared to meet any new experience when I'm willing to learn from someone who's already been through it.

"Listen to advice and accept instruction," Proverbs 19:20 urges, *"and in the end you will be wise" (NIV)*.

As the snowballs began to fly, I breathed a prayer of thanks for the wisdom gained from Janna's advice, Rose's instruction and God's incredible Word.

Snapshot 32

□

Letters from
a Friend

"I am sending you this notice in reply to your letter of Nov. 40, 1904. I realize of course that I am late in sending this and hope you will forgive my procrastination."

So began a letter I received while at band camp in 1971. Penned in bright blue ink, the writing filled the white space above a large green frog ogling a pink butterfly perched atop his nose. The writer was my friend, Beth Jones.

I recently found this letter, along with a stack of other mementos from my high school and college days, in a large brown box in my mother's basement.

Rereading the epistles Beth had sent me over a six-year period, I ran across such solemn and profound statements as:

• 1970. "In regards to your first card: ha, ha, tee hee, laugh, giggle, convulse, laugh some more, ha ha, thoroughly get hysterical, fall into the floor and laugh hard, bite my jaw from laughing so much, giggle. Actually, it wasn't all that funny."

• 1971. "It occurred to me while sitting here observing myself that I have a great and magnificent talent for combining a bunch of scattered pieces of nonsense and rabble into a neatly organized paragraph of nonsense and rabble."

• 1972. "At this eventful time in the history of our country, I am supplied with an immense cold which I casually and cordially caught from the one and only Richard [now her husband], Esquire. We both sniff, cough, and sneeze in concomitant rhythm. However, he has managed to keep a plain white nose while mine is a beacon in the dark."

• 1973? I was at college; she was living at home. "Would it be OK

77

if I send [younger brothers] Stevie and Jason down there for you to feed to the live football players?"

• 1975. "Guess what little old Suzy homemaker me did today! I made homemade rolls—ta-da! And after many years of practice, they might be edible and safe for humans."

Besides brightening my days, Beth's letters shared her deepest thoughts and feelings. She kept writing me and confiding in me during the college days when I was running headlong away from God—and from anyone who reminded me of him.

Usually, she simply told me the things God was doing in her life. Once she was bold enough to write, "I have never felt the need to pray for you so strongly. Nor have I felt the need to write you so much. . . . It seems like a great gulf has come between us."

For nearly two years, I scanned Beth's letters, tucked them away, and tried to forget them. But I didn't pitch them. And ultimately, God used those letters to help stir in me a longing for renewed relationships with my dear earthly friend and my only heavenly Father.

The summer after my sophomore year in college, Beth's prayers were answered. Like the prodigal son described by Jesus in Luke 15, I came to my senses. Realizing what a mess my life had become, I decided, *"I will get up and go"* back to God (v.18 NASU).

Unlike the older brother in Jesus' story, Beth stood right there beside our Father, watching and waiting, arms outstretched. With the Lord, she ran to embrace the wanderer returned.

I tossed most of the mementos I found in the brown box in my mother's basement. But I've kept several of Beth's letters. Some still make me laugh. Others remind me that a true friend will risk urging, "Hurry up and come home."

Snapshot 33

□

The Soybean Parable

Lately, I've been thinking a lot about soybeans. Maybe that's because my birthday's coming up—and it's one of those midlife birthdays.

Maybe that's because we drive past soybeans just about everywhere we go.

Maybe it's because of an incident that happened one October afternoon. My family and I were traveling along a county road past (you guessed it) a soybean field. Scanning row after row of brown, scraggly stems, one of our girls asked, "Why did the farmer let the soybeans die without harvesting them?"

"Those plants aren't dead," my husband Jerry replied. "They're just now ready to harvest." Then he asked, "Haven't you ever seen soybeans?"

"No," the girls answered.

Early in the summer, we'd watched rows of little green shoots emerge from the dark soil in numerous fields. During the weeks that followed, we passed plants growing taller and bushier until, finally, we couldn't see the soil any more, just a sea of green.

One day in mid-September, we noticed the formerly green seas had turned a breath-taking yellow. Afterward, the yellow faded into brown. The leaves fell away.

Yes, the girls had seen the plants in many stages. But they'd never seen the beans.

Jerry slowed the car and pulled to a stop beside the road. Stepping into the soybean field, he snapped off a piece of one plant. (Sorry, Mr. Farmer. We won't do it again.) Returning to his seat behind the wheel, he handed his prize back to the two girls.

"Cool," they said. Clinging to the stem of the plant were several

79

short, brown, fuzzy pods. Inside each pod were tiny, round, tan-yellow beans. While the girls shelled their beans into their laps, Jerry told them his favorite thing to do with soybeans: put them into a pea shooter and shoot them.

I had another idea: "Let's take these beans home and cook them."

"Mama!" the girls said, in a tone that meant, "How silly!" Little did they know that they had eaten soybeans numerous times. As babies, they drank soy-based formula to supplement their mama's milk. Now, they enjoy soybeans (or, to be more exact, soybean oil) whenever they eat margarine or salad dressing or anything made with shortening.

Soybeans also go to make things people don't eat—things like live-stock feed, paint, varnish and linoleum.

The girls didn't know such details and would have been less than interested if they had. They took their soybeans home and, acting on their daddy's suggestion, scouted around for a pea shooter. Meanwhile, I began reflecting on how many things come from a plant that appears to be dead.

A man named Abraham once *"faced the fact that his body was as good as dead" (Rom. 4:19 NIV)*. God had promised Abraham many descendants. Yet Abraham was 100 years old; his wife, 90; and they were childless.

The book of Romans tells us Abraham *"did not waver through unbelief regarding the promise of God"* but rather was *"fully persuaded"* it would come to pass (Rom. 4:20,21 NIV). Hebrews 11:12 announces, *"And so from this one man, and he as good as dead, came descendants as numerous as the stars in the sky and as countless as the sand on the seashore" (NIV)*.

Maybe Abraham and the soybeans have something to say to those among us who equate productivity with youth. Like the soybean, Abraham was fruitful long after anyone thought he could be—because he kept hanging in there, waiting for God to fulfill his intended purpose.

In seasons where we too may believe our usefulness has ended, may we learn to let God bring in the harvest in his time.

Snapshot 34

□

Biting the Bullet

In the days before children, my husband Jerry and I were moving into an almost-new house. As I vacuumed the carpet in the otherwise empty den, something began to clink-clink around the roller brush. Thinking I had picked up a stray straight pin or paper clip, I turned off my upright vacuum cleaner, hoisted it about a half-foot into the air, and shook it.

Nothing fell out. Deciding that whatever it was must have already gotten sucked up the hose, I lowered the vacuum and flipped the "on" switch again.

BOOM!

The explosion and my accompanying scream brought Jerry running from outside. He found me standing in the middle of the den, staring at the silent vacuum.

"What happened?" he yelled.

"I don't know," I wailed. "I just—what's that smell?"

We both sniffed. "Gunpowder?" I ventured.

Jerry picked up the vacuum. Onto the carpet rolled a spent .22 shell. I had shot my vacuum cleaner.

Happily, it didn't shoot me. Sadly, it didn't survive the bullet. We had a funeral—and then hurried out to replace the thing. No time to mourn when you have a house to vacuum before the furniture arrives.

In the years since, I've never murdered another appliance, though I've watched some of them die a slow death. And I've wanted to shoot some devices to put them out of their misery.

Right now, the first in line for the firing squad is our automatic dish-washer. The rotten contraption cleans so poorly that we pretty much have to wash the dishes before we wash them.

In our more honest moments, many of us would have to admit: we have a love-hate relationship with our conveniences. We love them when they really are convenient. We don't tell them enough, but we do love them.

And we hate it—even to the point of brief grief—when a particularly convenient convenience meets an untimely demise.

Oh, but we also hate it when something that is supposed to be a convenience proves an inconvenience instead. When the microwave takes longer to cook a frozen dinner than the oven, when the washing machine constantly gets its washload off balance and erupts into a grating BUZZZZZZZZZZ, when the fax machine will *not* send or receive the paper that must go *now,* we become a bit testy. Okay, we become really testy.

Thus, whether something we love conks without warning or something we hate limps along forever, we often develop "load rage." That is, the thing that was supposed to lighten our load has now increased it, and are we ever mad!

Ah, the cocked trigger of misplaced expectations, the carnage that ensues when we trust our load to things. God offers another option. Actually, he sings it to us in Psalm 81: *"Now I will relieve your shoulder of its burden; I will free your hands from their heavy tasks" (v. 6 NLT).*

What? Freedom from heavy tasks? Is the ancient God offering himself for use as another modern convenience?

Not exactly. We can't own God like we own a vacuum cleaner or a dishwasher. In order for him to lighten our load, in fact, he must own us. That is, we must choose to bind ourselves to him, listen to him, and follow him. We quit following our own desires and let him make the rules for our lives.

Doesn't make sense? You're right. God just doesn't sometimes.

When my vacuum cleaner bit the bullet, it bit the dust. Conversely, when we bite the bullet and willingly become tools in God's hands—he frees us from a life of hard labor. And he never limps or conks.

Snapshot 35

◻

People Don't Die

People don't die anymore. I have that on good authority. Excellent authority, actually.

I had graduated from college, but was not yet married, so we're talking mid-70s. Yes, that's quite a while ago. Ah, but this memory is vivid.

My newly married college roommate and her newly married husband invited me to visit them in Dallas, where Anna was working in a science lab and David was attending medical school. One day while Anna was working, I attended a class with David.

This class was not for sissies. We began in a theater-style room viewing larger-than-life slides of babies born with serious, deforming, often deadly diseases. This, of course, made me want to run out, get married, and have lots of children.

Everyone else looked at the slides attentively and jotted notes studiously. I closed my eyes a lot.

After this treat, we moved to a classroom setting, where the teacher who had shown the slides gave a lecture. I'm sure the lecture was wonderful, but I don't remember anything about it—until the professor blurted out the statement that has stayed with me to this day.

"People don't die anymore," he said. "That's why no one needs God."

Startled, I rechecked my ears: Had he really said what I thought he said? We'd just watched slides of babies who had died. The men and women sitting around me were training to be doctors because people get sick and have accidents and hurt each other, and—surely these students knew—in spite of the best medical treatment, folks don't always recover.

My brain confirmed: He really had said that people don't die anymore. According to his equation, longer life-spans equaled absence of death.

Glancing around the room, I expected to see surprised looks, smiles, and expressions of disbelief. Surely, someone would challenge, or at least question, such a statement. Or maybe the professor himself would break into a grin, showing us all he was joking.

But he wasn't joking. Straight-faced and earnest, he made his comment and moved on to his next point. Straight-faced, his students listened. Earnestly, they took notes.

What a shock! There I was, only half a day into med school, and I knew more than the lot of them. Not that I'm a genius, mind you. I simply didn't take the word of an expert when it contradicted the facts.

Death isn't fun to talk about or to face, but I'd say it's still just as real as ever. And for that very reason, may I suggest: We do need God.

The writer of Hebrews said, *"Man is destined to die once, and after that to face judgment" (9:27 NIV)*. Think through this with me. Based on your own observation, whose first statement is true: the now potentially deceased teacher who said, "People don't die," or the long-deceased writer of Hebrews, who affirmed that people do?

Consequently, whose second statement has more credibility?

If the Hebrews writer is on target, every felon who has met his demise has subsequently had a lot of explaining to do. Ah, but so will the rest of us. And frankly, it won't do us a bit of good to tally up the good we've done, hoping it outweighs the bad. The only explanation that carries any weight with the God of the Bible is, "Jesus."

So if you don't know Jesus intimately, I'd highly recommend your doing some serious reading, say, in the book of John; or if you like a mental challenge, Romans; or if you've caught wind of the *Left Behind* series, Revelation.

However, you can always do as I did with those slides of critically ill babies: take one good look at reality—and then close your eyes.

Snapshot 36

□

Long Distance

The call came one November morning while I was taking our daughters to school. Returning home, I listened to the message on the answering machine. Then I sat, staring through our south window at the weeping willow across the street.

My friend, Meta, had died of cancer two hours earlier.

When I could manage it, I called back to ask about the funeral arrangements. Then I wondered why I had made the call. Meta had lived in Mississippi; I lived a 10-hour drive away. After trying to figure out some way to make the trip, I realized it simply wouldn't work.

My husband had flown to Florida on business. He was staying two extra days to visit with his mom, whom he hadn't seen in months. Even if the cost weren't prohibitive, I couldn't very well kiss our 8- and 10-year old girls goodbye and hurry off to catch the next flight from Indianapolis to Memphis.

A cold north wind tousled the willow tree's wispy branches. But no flying carpet appeared to take me where I wanted to go. "Sometimes, living in a long-distance world stinks," I thought.

I had desperately wanted to see Meta in her last weeks, but that hadn't happened either. One night, unable to get her off my mind, I called. Expecting her husband to answer and explain, with profuse apologies, that she didn't feel up to talking, I was amazed when Meta herself picked up the phone. She was alone and feeling rather well. We talked more than an hour. It was almost like being there—but not quite. I didn't get to hug her or squeeze her hand or look her in the eye.

In today's mobile society, most of us experience the pain of living long-distance from people we love. Miles apart, we miss births, birthdays and other milestones. We communicate through cards and letters that rarely get written, phone calls that cost by the minute and e-mailed sentence fragments. We snatch hurried visits on holidays. We promise to get together more often. We lose touch.

Long-distance pain isn't new. In Old Testament days, Jacob had two wives, lots of property, and a passel of children. Yet, he kept looking west toward his father's house. He hadn't seen that house in 20 years. He'd missed his mama's funeral. He couldn't fly out to visit his dad for a weekend or even call to see how things were going. Finally, Jacob decided to gather his brood and go back.

Later, the apostle Paul wrote letters to his long-distance friends. More than once, he wrote, *"I long to see you" (Rom. 1:11; 2 Tim. 1:4 NIV).* Another time, he said, *"God can testify how I long for all of you with the affection of Christ Jesus" (Phil. 1:8 NIV).*

Like Jacob, Paul sometimes arranged to go to the people he longed to see. Other times, he could not. So he did something else that brought them near: he prayed for them.

The last time I prayed for Meta, I was sitting in my stuffed chair reading my Bible. It wasn't yet dawn. She kept coming to mind, so I began asking, "Father, fill her hospital room with your presence. Deliver her from her strong enemy, which is too mighty for her."

Later that same morning, after the phone call came, I sat staring south past the thrashing weeping willow—and realized two things. First, I had been crying out to God in Meta's behalf at the moment he delivered her. Second, I *will* look into her eyes again.

Because we both have confessed, "Jesus is Lord," it's just a matter of time till Meta and I have all eternity to sit and visit.

Snapshot 37

□

The Coat Hanger Conspiracy

Coat hangers are intelligent beings. They do, however, try to pretend they're inanimate objects. They want us to believe they're merely devices around which a garment is draped for hanging from a hook or rod.

But I know the truth. I've watched them. I've wrestled with them. At times, I've been defeated by them. (Muzzle that smile. This confession does not come easily for me.)

The coat hangers in our closets and laundry room hold all manner of clothing items, in addition to coats. At any given time, various hangers hold nothing. They are supposedly available for those clothes that have been in use or have just come out of the wash and need to be hanged.

I say "supposedly available" for two reasons. In the first place, coat hangers have a maddening habit of multiplying and vanishing. Unfortunately, you never know which approach they're going to take, but you can always reckon you'll either (a) not be able to find a hanger at all or (b) have way too many extras.

This would be okay if, once you found a coat hanger, you could actually use it. But the one thing these little creatures love more than multiplying and vanishing is conspiring.

Here's what happens, based on pictures from secret surveillance cameras: Several neatly hung hangers see a hand coming toward them. Somehow, they know precisely which hanger that hand will grab. In the second before the "snatch," the hangers intertwine so that the chosen hanger is inextricably linked to several others. No amount of creative jiggling will free this hanger—until the unwitting person decides to give up and select a different one. Immediately, the holding hangers release the held hanger, and it plunges to the floor. The others then regroup, latching onto a different hanger just as the person's hand reaches to grasp it.

Okay, so I made up the part about the surveillance cameras, and the "intelligent beings" business is iffy, too. But what irritates me so much about coat hangers is that they irritate me so much. So maybe you can understand why I was perplexed the day I stood in our laundry room, yanking on a hopelessly tangled hanger, and the word "thanksgiving" came to mind.

"It's not Thanksgiving," I muttered. Then, a surprising idea barreled in like a bumper car, knocking my mutter out of the way: "Thanksgiving isn't a day. It isn't even an attitude. Thanksgiving is an action."

I cannot ever recall a time when thoughts of coat hangers caused a deep sense of gratitude to well up in me. At that moment, I certainly did not feel thankful for them. And I had no desire to recall the verse from Ephesians 5 that came to mind anyway, urging, *"Always give thanks for everything to God the Father in the name of our Lord Jesus Christ" (v. 20 NLT).*

Frustrated, I let go of the uncooperative hanger. It clattered to the floor. Since God had me over a barrel, using scripture and all, I reluctantly told him, "Thank you for coat hangers." Trying another hanger, I added, "Thank you for closets with clothes in them—and for pieces of wire and plastic that do help keep clothes available and neat. Thank you that you provide these hangers: We rarely have to buy them."

By then I was on a roll. "Thank you for arms to reach for hangers and hands to grasp them. Thank you for the family members who wear the clothes these hangers hold."

Funny thing: By the time I finished saying, "Thank you," I was truly thankful.

Snapshot 38

□

Technology's to Blame

It's technology's fault. If we didn't have fax machines, answering machines, portable phones, cell phones, modems, computers, minivans, 18-wheelers, tractors, buses, trains, planes, toaster ovens, microwaves, TVs, radios, CD players, DVD players, vacuum cleaners and power tools, we'd all live pure, wholesome lives—like the Unabomber.

We'd walk most places. (Of course, my family would have to leave on Saturday night to get to church by Sunday morning.) We would ride only bicycles—which might put the tiniest cramp into holiday travel and vacation plans. Of course, if we wanted to sneak across country and blow someone up, then we could make an exception and fly in an airplane.

We'd never again use guns to kill. Clubs and knives, maybe, but never guns. We'd use bombs only to destroy really bad guys—like store owners and office workers. And then we'd use only handmade bombs created from natural ingredients.

I've long suspected it's my computer's fault that I yell at my children. It's the automatic dishwasher that has kept me from communicating on a deeper level with my husband. If we didn't have indoor plumbing, we'd have more friends. They would come to our house often because, every time nature called, nature's what they'd get to enjoy, even in blizzards and thunderstorms.

When the earth was new and no scientist or computer whiz had yet been born, people lived in a garden. They ate fresh fruits and vegetables. They faced no rush hour traffic, no mail fraud, no office politics. They got to spend time with God daily. And they weren't in a rush to get through it. In fact, it was the time of day they looked forward to the most.

The rest of the day, they didn't sit around watching soap operas or reading the newspaper. They worked the garden. Their labor was good—satisfying and challenging—not the grinding, crushing work that farming has been ever since. The weather always favored them. The crops never failed. Their pay was more than adequate and the benefits, unbelievably generous.

Then, the man found some stray parts and wires and made a radio. Suddenly, the idyllic setting was shattered. Loud music drowned out the songs of birds. Talk shows blared on and on through the long summer afternoons. The man began longing for a telephone, so he could call in, ask the talk show host an impressive question and hear himself on radio. He neglected his work in order to build that phone. When it was completed, the woman wanted to use it first to call her friend in the next garden. Marital discord was born.

Wait. Back up. That's not how it happened. Blessed with a perfect setting unmarred by any hint of modern technology, the woman and the man made a choice that every person since has repeated. They did wrong. Specifically, they ate the one fruit God had told them not to eat.

I'm sure the fruit was organically grown. But it was off-limits. By indulging in the one thing they'd been denied, they ruined everything—the world, their lives, their relationship with each other, their relationship with God.

Today, we could gather all our technological goodies into a heap and burn them. But before we'd even get the fire put out, someone would have done something to mess up our pure, new world. Only as we yield to the One *"who created the heavens and stretched them out, who spread out the earth and its offspring, who gives breath to the people on it, and spirit to those who walk in it" (Isa. 42:5 NASU)* will we see beauty and purity return.

Snapshot 39

□

Sewer Troubles

You know you're in trouble when you're washing your hands in the restroom at church and turn to find sewer water, complete with black smut, rising from the drain in the floor behind you.

In such a moment, you might think, not of high and lofty things like the Sunday morning worship service about to start, but of baser things like tearing out of the bathroom and down the hall to summon help. After calling the cavalry, you'd likely assume you can leave the problem behind.

Silly you.

Two days after your first encounter of the grossest kind, you're in another church in another town. You enter the facilities to change clothes before a long drive. Immediately, you notice: the room smells, more than most. A person who's exiting warns of water on the floor from a toilet that's overflowed. You begin to wonder if you've stumbled upon an epidemic of church sewer problems.

Carefully completing your change of clothing, you drive to a campground in yet another part of the state. The room assigned to you has—you guessed it—sewer problems: water on bathroom floor, toilet won't flush.

You change rooms. The facilities work! Ah, but your relief is short-lived. The next day in the building where your meeting is held, the commode quits working. In the cafeteria restroom, two of four others go on the blink.

By now, you're thinking, "Wait a minute. This story is getting too far-fetched." And it would be—except that it happened. By Thursday of that sewer-plugged week, I wasn't sure whether the problem was (a) universal or (b) me. But now I know: You don't appreciate waste removal systems till you don't have them.

Let's face it, who ever heard of a "bathroom appreciation month"? And consider garbage—a subject about which most of us rarely think. My husband thinks about it, but only because his company makes components for garbage trucks, more properly called "refuse equipment."

It's possible that you know your mail carrier, but how many of you know your garbage man? Has the idea ever crossed your mind to thank him or her? I suspect not. But what if the refuse truck never came? What if you yourself had to figure out what to do with the tons of garbage you and your family generate?

A frightening thought.

Worse yet, what if you never took advantage of the waste removal systems you have? Never took out the garbage. Never flushed the commode. Before long, your neighbors would have something to say about that. And your house would—well, we can only imagine.

But interestingly enough, we have a waste removal system most of us aren't using. It's a God-given system to remove the filth, not from our buildings, but from our lives. It's called *confession*.

The key to this system is simple: When your thoughts, attitudes, words or actions are wrong, call them what God calls them and ask him to pitch them.

Simple? Yes. Easy? No.

Ever since the first people walked the earth, we've been trying to hedge with God and camouflage our dirty deeds with respectable words. For example, what God calls "resentment" we might call "hurt feelings." What God labels "obscene" we might label "adult." What God terms "debt" we might term "credit."

We all produce lots of waste. But even in church circles, we've quit flushing. Consequently, sewer water, with black smut and unmistakable odor, rises around us. It may be ankle-, knee- or even waist-deep. Yet we don't see that we're in trouble.

Ah, but *"if we admit our sins—make a clean breast of them . . . He'll forgive our sins and purge us of all wrongdoing"* (1 John 1:9 MSG).

□

Society for the Prevention of Bursting Balloons

Some situations call for action.

One Friday night after a women's conference, sitting in my car, waiting for a more learned driver to lead me to the hotel, I witnessed one such situation.

The group sponsoring the conference had placed bunches of balloons outside the building to notify the attendees, "This is the place!" With the meeting adjourned, the balloons were no longer needed. A woman (most surely, a committee member) came outside, untied the string holding one bunch of the balloons, wrapped her arms around a balloon—and popped it. Methodically and without the slightest hint of compassion, she proceeded to pop each of the remaining balloons.

I couldn't watch. It was difficult even to listen. No, I didn't leap from the vehicle and throw myself between the woman and the balloons. I sat idly by while, repeatedly, what had been filled and buoyant became instantly limp and lifeless. That night, I did make a commitment to start an organization needed far too long. Its name sprang full-blown to my lips: The Society for the Prevention of Bursting Balloons.

I've had a soft spot for balloons ever since I can remember. If one ever comes into my possession, it will generally remain with me until it has shriveled into a lopsided grape. It's not that I love balloons that much. It's that I detest popping them. (Question for discussion: Have you ever tried to put a balloon in the garbage without popping it?)

A couple of years ago, I attended another conference where balloons were treated cruelly. In a class designed to stretch our creativity, we were to blow up a balloon, draw a face on it, then sit on it and pop it. I obediently complied with the first three steps. Unfortunately, I sat on the balloon so tentatively that it sort of flattened and pooched out the sides instead of popping. Pretty creative, don't you think? The last I saw that balloon, it had a very long face.

Now that I've seen the wholesale slaughter of unsuspecting balloons, I've decided it's time to organize. Together, the Society for the Prevention of Bursting Balloons will march under a banner declaring, "We are the SPoBBs!" We'll picket, lifting signs that demand, "Stop that Pop!" And, "Wait! Don't Deflate!"

We'll work tirelessly to keep balloons away from conferences, toddlers, males of any age, ceiling fans, kittens, straight pins, and cacti. We will patrol birthday parties and county fairs, keeping accurate counts of all balloons on premises and making sure that not a single one bites the dust. We will be zealous and unflagging in our efforts.

All the major news media will cover us. Someone will build a monument to us. We'll get thank-you cards from millions of children and hate mail from millions of moms. We may even win the Nobel Peace Prize. In the end, we will have spent a huge amount of time and effort accomplishing absolutely nothing of consequence . . .

Some situations call for action.

And by far the most significant of those situations have to do with people, not things. In Proverbs 31:8–9, a wise mom told her son, *"Speak up for those who have no voice, for the justice of all who are dispossessed. Speak up, judge righteously, and defend the cause of the oppressed and needy"* (HCSB).

Okay, forget the balloons. But if you see a person being sat on, deflated or destroyed, please don't sit idly by. Don't wait to form a society or for someone else to stand up for what is right. You may be the one person who can make a difference. So do something that matters. Speak up.

Snapshot 41

□

Letter to a Bosnian Mother

Dear mother,

You don't know me, and I don't know your name. But I care about you and your baby.

I'm sending the things in this shoe box as a result of reading a children's book. A friend let me borrow the book to read to my two daughters. Actually, the girls read it to me.

Megan and Amanda are 10 and 8 years old now. Snuggling together in the bed in Megan's room, we started the story, Miracle in a Shoe Box. *The man who wrote it, Franklin Graham, is head of an international Christian relief organization called Samaritan's Purse.*

It's a good thing the girls were doing the reading. Glimpsing the loss families are facing because of the war in your country, I struggled to hold back the tears—and finally just let them flow.

When the girls learned they could each send a shoe box filled with gifts to a child in Bosnia, they couldn't wait to do so. Each chose several items for a girl her own age.

"Mama, can I send a box to a baby, too?" Megan asked.

"We'll all do it together," I answered.

We hope you like the new blanket and rattle and socks. But of all the things we placed in the box, my favorite is the delicate white, hand-crocheted cap and sweater set. It's not new. And it won't keep your baby very warm. But it's the kind of thing every mother delights to see her infant daughter wearing.

The girls' grandmother (my husband's mom) made the set for Megan before she was born. She, and then Amanda, wore it for special occasions.

Of course, my daughters have long since outgrown the set, but when

I gave all their other baby clothes away, I kept it. I thought I might save it for the daughters they may have someday. But somewhere in the middle of a children's book about a shoe box, God showed me he wanted me to give this cap and sweater to you.

When I took them from the closet where they were stored, they had a few yellowed places. I washed them carefully. Still wet, the tiny items looked fluffy and fresh and brilliantly white. Holding them up, I pictured the two babies who used to wear them.

Those babies weren't born into the tragedy of war. Even today, neither they nor I can begin to grasp the pain you and your child have experienced. But I think I understand something of the hopes and dreams for your daughter that must ache inside you right now. I ached for my babies too. And I prayed for them to the God who revealed himself in Jesus Christ.

Jesus' story is the Christmas story. He was born to struggling parents in a turbulent time. As far as we know, his mother had no socks or rattle or cap or sweater to give him—just cloths she wrapped around him. When he grew up, people declared war on him, saying they were doing it in the name of God. He let them kill him, because in his death lay the only opportunity for my girls and me and you and your baby to have real, abundant, never-ending life.

Before my girls were born, I found a promise in the Bible to which I've clung. It says, "Your children shall be disciples—taught of the Lord [and obedient to His will]; and great shall be the peace and undisturbed composure of your children" (Isa. 54:13 AMP).

May the third child to wear this sweater and cap also know him who alone gives peace.

> *With love,*
> *A mother like you*

Snapshot 42

□

Facing into the Wind

Here I sit, watching snow hurtle sideways past my window, dark clouds scuttling overhead. A few minutes ago, the sun was shining brightly. A few minutes before that, it was snowing and blowing.

Last Tuesday, temperatures climbed into the 70s here in central Indiana. I went walking in shorts. That was before the thermometer fell to 14 degrees on Wednesday night.

I think we're living on a weather yo-yo. Yes, I know we are: the sun's out again.

The culprit in much of the weather madness around here is something I cannot see and did not factor into our decision to move to the Midwest. I expected cold. I rather looked forward to seeing snow. But no one warned me about the wind. Yes, I knew about windy Chicago and windy Kansas and even windy Dallas, having visited Texas a couple of times.

But somehow I failed to make the connection that Indiana, like those other places, consists mainly of flat terrain. With nothing to stand in its way, the wind blows where it will. More often than not, it blows hard.

It tumbles trash cans and rolls them into streets. It sends trash into neighboring counties. It makes great trees sway ominously and our curb-side mailbox dance on its pole. It gives my girls headaches when they try to play outside, and it blows weather systems through here so fast you miss them if you blink.

Speaking of which, it's snowing again. It's snowing furiously, wet flakes hurled sideways as if by some unseen hand. We've had a good bit of snow this winter, but I can't remember when I've actually seen snow falling down. Usually, it's flying by—thanks to the wind.

A man named Job once felt he was being hurled about like flying snow or scattered trash. Having suffered a host of tragedies, including the loss of his health and the deaths of all his children, Job told the Lord: *"You snatch me up and drive me before the wind; you toss me about in the storm" (Job 30:22 NIV).*

I walk in local neighborhoods. On those all-too-frequent wintry windy days, I often turn a corner, only to find myself facing into a stiff wind. Now, the wind hasn't yet snatched me up and tossed me about, but it does take my breath away. It fights against me, slowing my pace. It makes me wish I were home curled up under an afghan in a cozy chair.

When I'm walking, an opposing wind can defeat me, but if I were piloting an airplane, I would taxi to the end of the runway and turn the plane directly into the wind. In the world of airplanes, it's the wind blowing against me, combined with a powerful engine and sturdy wings, that gives the lift needed to fly.

At one time or another, most of us have felt buffeted by the winds of God. Like Job, we often mistakenly feel that God is trying to beat us down when, in reality, his desire is to lift us up.

Isaiah 40:31 promises: *"Those who hope in the Lord will renew their strength. They will soar on wings like eagles" (NIV).* Psalm 104:3 says that the God of the Bible *"rides on the wings of the wind" (NIV).* During hard times, he is circling above, waiting for the precise moment when we finally grow weary of being buffeted.

When at last we lift our eyes and cry to him, he swoops down under us and lifts us. Heading into the wind, he carries us. Only then do we realize that what we thought was blowing against us is what has enabled us to soar.

Snapshot 43

□

Crying the Blues

It creeps up on you when you least suspect it. Then it pounces—and grabs, holding you in its deadlock grip. While you flail and beg for release, it knocks you flat and sits atop you. While you struggle for breath, it laughs.

Depression is merciless. It may hit because you can't go home for the holidays—or *because* you're going home for the holidays. It may accompany illness or loss. It may ride in on the darkness of increasingly shorter days. It may march where you have fallen, tramping across your failures, shouting repeatedly, "You're a loser!" or "Things will never change. You'll have to live like this for the rest of your life!"

Depression likes to doodle in the dust of your dreams. When experience crashes short of expectation, depression enjoys playing in the debris. It can thrive on everyone else's despondency. It can thrive on everyone else's cheer.

Sometimes, it's a conjurer, creating the illusion of failure when you have not failed. Sometimes, it's a pick-pocket, robbing you of joy when, outwardly, everything's going well. Always, it's heavy, paralyzing and suffocating.

We can invite depression, and sometimes we do. We dig our own pit, jump into it, and then feel deeply despondent about the place we find ourselves. Other times, the pit opens earthquake-like, before us, even when we're trying to walk the right path.

Depression is a conundrum. It may spring from physical, emotional, or spiritual causes. Often, it arises from some combination of the three.

When one poet found himself depressed, he didn't attempt to hide his feelings. What's more, he didn't attempt to hide the sense of betrayal he felt. *"I counted on you, God. Why did you walk out on me?"* he asked *(Psalm 43:2 MSG).*

But the poet didn't stop there. Three times in two songs he confronted his depression and identified the one step that would break despondency's deadlock grip: *"Why are you down in the dumps, dear soul? Why are you crying the blues? Fix my eyes on God"* (Psalm 42:5,11; 43:5 MSG).

That solution may sound simplistic. In reality, it's practical.

When a depressed person seeks medical help, the doctor may do a physical exam, ask questions, and call upon expertise gained through education and practice. Through it all, he's seeking to solve a riddle that includes both cause and cure. Yet, even the best physician can miss the mark as easily as hit it.

The God the psalmist worshiped knows everything about each of us. He doesn't have to do any guessing to pinpoint the sources of depression. And because he loves us so completely, he doesn't hesitate to let us know what needs to be done to correct it.

When a king named Saul nursed depression, God announced the root cause: Saul's own rebellion and arrogance. Saul never did yield to God. Consequently, he never did conquer depression.

When a truth-speaker named Elijah grew depressed, God knew the man was exhausted. To begin lifting Elijah's spirits, God prescribed two good naps and two good meals.

Crying out to the same God, the poet found he had a different need, a need to drag his thoughts from the gutter and fling them toward the skies. He told God, *"When my soul is in the dumps, I rehearse everything I know of you"* (Psalm 42:6 MSG).

Depression is a conundrum, but God has never met a riddle he can't solve. Depression is a conjurer and a pick-pocket, but God is a restorer of stolen hope. Depression is merciless, but God is merciful. When we fix our eyes on him, overwhelming victory is ours through him.

Snapshot 44

□

Do the
Next Thing

A friend of mine is smack in the middle of a mess. Her family is falling apart. The home she's worked so hard to build lies in shambles.

Now, mind you, this friend is a woman of faith. You couldn't have looked at her life three years ago and predicted this would happen. You couldn't look back now and find seriously dumb choices that have landed her where she is. Yet, here she is, entering the workforce in midlife (by necessity, not choice), returning to school, living below the poverty level and facing a new crisis daily.

One day, she and I were talking. She was telling me a bit about the newest hits she was taking, and it fell to me to respond. I wanted to be an encourager, but I had no words. I knew that a pat on the head and a brisk, "Don't worry, honey; everything will be all right," just wasn't going to cut it.

The one thing that did come to mind didn't seem appropriate. It wasn't a heart-warming adage or a hope-inspiring sentiment. It was more like a four-word command. And yet those four words had really helped another woman in an overwhelming situation, and they had helped me.

I'd read them in a book—or maybe I heard them on a tape. Either way, a woman named Elisabeth Elliott was recounting her experience of being widowed while in her 20s. During the days when she was dealing with fresh grief, trying to rear a baby daughter, and carrying on mission work in the jungle of Ecuador, someone suggested this key to coping without caving:

Do the next thing.

That doesn't sound awfully profound. But for me, at least, it hit and stuck. You see, I can be overwhelmed by far fewer demands than either

Elisabeth Elliott or my friend have faced. I'm overwhelmed, not only when crises mount, but also when responsibilities or even opportunities seem to shoot upward like Jack's beanstalk.

To some, the overwhelming may be exhilarating. But for me, the overwhelming is paralyzing. Put too much on my plate and I can't eat any of it. Send too many logs down my little stream and they jam.

Knowing my need to overcome the paralysis of the overwhelming, I began to practice that simple advice. I found that doing the next thing is like getting to the part in *Heidi* when the crippled girl takes her first shaky step. To someone who didn't know better, that step would seem insignificant. But to a previously paralyzed person, it's breakthrough.

To do the next thing, I have to *identify* the next thing. That's one place where it helps immeasurably to know God. Since he always guides in the right direction, I find it vital to ask, "Lord, what is the next thing?"

I may not see the sense in his answer. But that's okay. Proverbs 20:24 reminds me, *"How can we understand the road we travel? It is the Lord who directs our steps" (NLT).* Trapped in a logjam, my job is not to understand the next thing, but to do it.

Of course, my logjams don't begin to compare with my friend's paralyzing problems. Still, I mustered the courage to ask, "Would it help if I told you: 'Do the next thing'?"

She paused. I waited. "I can't begin to see the end of this awful mess," she said. "I don't want to think where all this is going to take me. But yes," she concluded, with a new hint of hope in her voice, "I can do the next thing."

Snapshot 45

□

I Will Sing

Ever read something that drew back and slapped you?

Recently, I ran across three little words that slapped me, sent me sprawling and jumped up and down on top of me—in a helpful sort of way, of course.

You'll never guess them, so I'll tell you.

"I will sing."

That's it. "I will sing."

Seems like a pretty tame phrase to you, doesn't it? Well, notice that it doesn't say, "I feel like singing." This little phrase involves choice. In saying it, I'm announcing that my will is going to overrule my emotions. Regardless how I feel, I will sing.

Notice, too that it doesn't say, "I may sing," or "I will consider singing," or even, "I will make melody in my heart." These three words involve action. To carry them out, I have to open mouth, exert breath and make sounds that at least somewhat resemble notes and melodies. Lyrics are helpful, as well.

The day I read these words, I determined to adopt them—for the very reason that I didn't feel like singing. Driving home from an out-of-town appointment after dark, I started tentatively at first. Frankly, it took great effort both to sing and to listen to myself.

"In a cavern, in a canyon," I warbled, "excavating for a mine, dwelt a miner, forty-niner, and his daughter Clementine."

Proceeding through all the verses I could recall, I decided that "Clementine" is both sad and silly. "Drove she ducklings to the water every morning just at nine. Struck her foot upon a splinter, fell into the foaming brine."

And the real tear-jerker: "Ruby lips above the water" (in childhood, one of my sisters thought that was "groovy lips," which lets you know the era we grew up in) "blowing bubbles soft and fine. Alas for me I was no swimmer, so I lost my Clementine."

By the end of the song, I was—no, not sobbing—singing with gusto. Assorted other songs followed, many of them dredged up from childhood. Alongside ditties like, "Oh, What a Beautiful Morning" (sung at approximately 9:03 P.M.), I found myself belting out hymns and choruses.

"Jesus wants me for a sunbeam to shine for him each day." "Climb, climb up sunshine mountain, heavenly breezes blow." "I will sing of the goodness of the Lord forever; I will sing; I will sing."

Launching into that last chorus, I recalled the whole sentence that contains my adopted phrase. It's the first verse of Psalm 101, and it says, *"I will sing of your love and justice; to you, O Lord, I will sing praise" (NIV)*.

That reminded me of perhaps the strangest battle strategy of all time. The good king in this battle was named Jehoshaphat. His country faced attack by three enemy nations whose combined forces far outnumbered Jehoshaphat's troops.

Jehoshaphat drew up his battle plans this way: He called a day of prayer in which he and the people cried out to God. After praying, Jehoshaphat took the counsel, not of a general, but of a prophet. Marshalling his troops, he instructed singers—yes, singers—to lead the charge.

While marching toward the enemy armed with nothing we would consider a weapon, the singers did not sing "Clementine." At God's command, they sang praises to him. While they sang, God ambushed the attacking armies so that they destroyed each other.

Silly songs may brighten my mood. But if my life reflects the humility, faith and obedience of Jehoshaphat, the songs that honor God will invite him into the battle on my behalf. So, hey, I *will* sing—especially when I don't feel like it.

◼

Off the Hook

Where would we be without the miracle of the modern fax? The miracle for me is: sometimes the fax works. Too often when I'm involved, it doesn't.

Like the time when I needed to fax an article to the newspaper.

I did all the normal things: turned on the computer, entered my word processing program, and started writing. When the manuscript was flawless (well, okay—when I couldn't figure out anything else to fix), I clicked the Print button, told the computer to print to the fax and specified where to send the fax. The computer did as it was told, but when it dialed the newspaper fax number, I heard a busy signal coming from the recesses of the computer tower. Apparently, the newspaper fax line was sending or receiving another fax.

While waiting to try again, I decided to play with the buttons at the top of the fax screen. This was my first mistake. Click. "Let's see what this does." Click. "And this." When I clicked the "Manual Receive" button, the trouble started.

Inside the computer tower, I heard a dial tone, followed by shrill fax-receive tones. But, alas, there was no incoming fax to receive. *Oh, no,* I thought. Frantically, I clicked off the "Manual Receive" button.

This was my second mistake. After a few seconds, the grating female voice every telephone user knows spoke from the depths of my computer tower: "If you need to make a call, please hang up and try again." She repeated her instructions three times. Then my computer erupted into those deafening beeps that alert you your phone is off the hook. Trying to silence the beeps, I punched more buttons. At last, the computer tower fell silent.

Relieved, I tried once again to fax my article to the newspaper. A message appeared on my screen informing me my modem was missing.

"Oh, no!" I cried. "I've killed my modem!"

Panic-stricken, I tried basic modem resuscitation techniques, including going to the icon marked "Control Panel" and trying to figure out what to do next, punching the computer reset button, and shaking my head in disbelief. All I got for my effort were more messages telling me my modem could not be located.

Breathing a prayer for help, I decided to call my husband Jerry at work. Maybe the techy guys in his office would know what to do. I picked up the telephone. The line was dead. In fact, every phone in the house was dead. Not only had I killed my modem, I'd destroyed our entire phone system.

Or maybe not. Maybe the modem was simply off the hook. But if so, I wondered: *How does one hang up a phone embedded in the guts of a computer?*

Thanks to a cell phone and a coworker of Jerry's named Rick, I found out: One turns off the computer, waits 10 or 15 seconds, and then restarts the computer. (All us computer whizzes know reset buttons don't give modems time to reset themselves.)

Okay, okay, so I'm not a computer whiz—even though I've been using computers long enough that I should be. And though I've only left my modem off the hook once, I seem to leave my mind off the hook regularly.

The miracle is: The times I'm most disconnected, God reminds me what he said in 2 Corinthians 12:9. *"My grace is enough; it's all you need. My strength comes into its own in your weakness" (MSG).*

Snapshot 47

□

View from the Top

It was an impressive sight. Standing on the second floor of the more-than-century-old Indiana state house, I stared upward in awe. From my position in an open area at the center of the building, I could gaze up past towering marble statues and columns, past ornate chandeliers, old wood and hand-painted trim on the third and fourth floors, to the stained-glass mosaic that fills the giant dome.

I was helping chaperone a fourth-grade field trip. The ten-year-olds standing around me were enjoying the view above as much as I. "Look! Wow!" they exclaimed, their heads thrown back, their eyes wide.

After touring the state house and eating lunch at a nearby McDonald's, the group trekked to one of the tallest buildings in Indianapolis, the Bank One tower. There, we rode the express elevator to the 48th floor, filed into a long conference room with a wall of windows, and stared out on the city from above.

In the streets far below, we saw cars that looked toy-size. In the distance, we spied a section of the speedway where the Indianapolis 500 race is held. Closer by, partially blocked by another building, we located the Indiana state house.

"That's where we were?" the children asked in disbelief. I understood their doubt. Although still a stately building, the capitol didn't look nearly as impressive from our perch 48 stories up.

In fact, it looked rather little. The outside of the dome was painted green. We could see nothing of the stained glass, the chandeliers or the marble statues we knew were inside.

"It's all a matter of perspective," I thought. Then, I realized the same is true of a lot of things in life.

From where most of us stand, for example, the giant corporations, the imposing institutions and the major governments of the world seem as high above us as the stained glass in that state-house dome. The heads of these entities tower like the elevated marble statues. We may look up to such important people with awe that borders on worship. "Look! Wow!" we exclaim, our heads thrown back, our eyes wide.

But God has another perspective. Ephesians 1:21 says Jesus is *"far above any ruler or authority or power or leader or anything else in this world"* (NLT). And Christ himself taught us to pray to *"our Father in heaven"* (Matt. 6:9 NLT).

Like the bank executives who usually meet in that top-floor conference room, God is used to looking down on everyone we're accustomed to looking up to. He regards as unimpressive the people and things that so easily impress us.

And like the youngsters in that fourth-grade class, you and I can experience the incredible privilege of looking out on life from God's perspective. It doesn't happen automatically, though.

Rather, it takes a willingness to enter into God himself and let him whisk us up to his vantage point. It takes a daily act of pondering the pages of a book we call the Bible. And it takes an eagerness to cultivate what only God can give—the ability to see what lies before us with the eyes of faith.

Snapshot 48

□

Rock, Ice, Bridge

It may be a fine distinction. But somehow, it's an important one. And though it has nothing to do with bridge crossing, ice walking and back diving—it has everything to do with them.

Let's start by walking on ice, so to speak. Many years ago, I heard a wise man say that faith is only as strong as its object. He gave an illustration I've never forgotten. Suppose you walk out on an ice-covered lake. What determines whether you take a really cold dip? The strength of your faith? No. The strength of the ice.

You can stride confidently onto thin ice—and go under. You can crawl fearfully onto solid ice—and stay up. A little faith goes a long way, if it's well-placed.

Now imagine yourself in mountainous terrain, peering over the edge of a cliff. Before you stretches a swinging bridge. Below the bridge—way below—lie sharp rocks and a winding stream. Suppose you step onto the bridge. What determines whether you take a quick trip to the rocks? The strength of your faith? No. The strength of the bridge.

In both cases, faith is putting your full weight on something. If your faith is misplaced, you've welcomed tragedy. If your faith is well-placed, you've welcomed victory.

Now, let's say you've tested the ice and the bridge time and again. Always, they've proven trustworthy. Not once has either given you the slightest reason to doubt its dependability. Once again, it's time to step out. You do so, but not with confidence, rather with deep fear that this time what you're relying on will let you down.

You're demonstrating faith. Well-placed faith. But not trust.

Like I said, it's a fine distinction. But for me, it's become a significant one. I like to think of it as a back-diving issue. In my childhood, it took intense effort on my mom's part to get me to take the faith step of putting my face under water. After that, I loved swimming.

It took more intense effort on Mama's part to get me to take the faith step of diving. After that, I loved diving. But I never could trust my mom enough to do a back dive. Standing backward on the edge of the diving board, arms above my head, back arched, I just knew that if I kept going backward, I'd circle right into that diving board.

No matter how many times I saw my mom or my sister arch backward into the water, never getting near the board, I couldn't bring myself to do what they were doing.

But, okay, back diving isn't the issue. And the one I'm having trouble trusting isn't my mom. As a child of eight, I placed the full weight of my life onto Jesus Christ. In the years since, I've tested him time and again. Always, he's proven trustworthy. Not once has he given me the slightest reason to doubt his dependability.

Yet, I've continued to take each step with great apprehension, as if God were thin ice or a rickety bridge. Suddenly I see: Faith is stepping out onto the bridge. Trust is doing so with confidence and a calm expectation that the bridge will hold.

In the Old Testament, a man named Isaiah said to God, *"You will keep in perfect peace all who trust in you, whose thoughts are fixed on you!"* Then, Isaiah said to us, *"Trust in the Lord always, for the Lord God is the eternal Rock"* *(Isa. 26:3–4 NLT).*

Now that I see the distinction, it's time for me to raise my arms, lean back, and trust.

Snapshot 49

□

April Morning

Tragedy shouldn't happen in April. April heralds newness. With daylight now longer than darkness, with warmth infiltrating chill, with the new green of budding trees and bushes overruling the brown of empty branches, April sings of spring.

Yes, April has its showers (as well as its thunderstorms). Occasionally, even in the South, April has its unexpected snows. I can remember playing in a ground-covering snow one April afternoon during my college days at the University of Mississippi.

But no matter what kinds of showers this month may bring, the mention of "April" tends to conjure images of days like the one unfolding as I write. The wide sky, the high sun, the spirited breezes cry, "Come out! Enjoy!"

In a few minutes, I'll go. The breeze tickling my face, the sun flinging its shadow over my shoulder, the sky daring me to find a cloud, I'll take a walk in a world celebrating life. I'll bask in the beauty—but I won't be taken in by it.

Tragedies do happen in April.

April 12, 1945, Franklin D. Roosevelt looked out on a clear sky from the Little White House in Warm Springs, Georgia, where he'd gone to spend two restful weeks. Visibly sick with heart disease, Roosevelt was seeking the same recuperative strength he'd found in Warm Springs years earlier, when first stricken with polio.

Just starting his fourth term as President, Roosevelt had led the U.S. to the brink of an Allied victory in World War II. But he never saw the victory. He never even saw the end of April 12. He died that day of a cerebral hemorrhage.

April 19, 1970, my parents, sisters, brother and I attended church and then ate at a local restaurant, as usual for a Sunday. We drove home from the restaurant in the midst of a wild downpour. On reaching home, we began to hear the ambulances.

While we were eating, a tornado had touched down just blocks from where we sat. Ripping its way through Corinth, Mississippi, the tornado leveled several churches and hundreds of homes, killing five people and injuring many others.

April 21, 1988, I was working in the loft office in our house in Corinth, enjoying the sun that streamed through the double window near my desk. The phone rang. "Deborah," my mother said, "Grandmother Brown has died."

I wasn't surprised by the call. My maternal grandmother had been critically ill for several months. Like FDR's body, hers gave up on her, in spite of all doctors could do. All these years later, I still feel the loss.

April 19, 1995, a bomb tore through the Alfred P. Murrah Federal Building in Oklahoma City, stunning the nation and devastating thousands. Two years later in April, we faced the first trials of Timothy McVeigh and Terry Nichols, two men later convicted in the bombing.

We're kidding ourselves if we think April skies will deflect all hurts. This globe and all who live on it are in bondage to decay, no matter what the month.

But a visionary named John has written of a time when heaven and earth will be "new-created." He describes that time in the last pages of the Bible: *"Look! Look! God has moved into the neighborhood, making his home with men and women! They're his people, he's their God. He'll wipe every tear from their eyes. Death is gone for good—tears gone, crying gone, pain gone" (Rev. 21:1,3–4 MSG).*

Some days, April's song may seem only a cruel irony. But if, in the beauty of an April morning, we see a picture of a time when God will make all things new, we're embracing a hope that will not disappoint.

Snapshot 50

◻

Let's Pause

The late afternoon sun fell heavy on the flowering trees that dotted the Ball State University campus. I needed to finish my errand and get home to fix supper. But something in me refused to be hurried.

Maybe it was the long shadows that made me want to slow down. Maybe it was the perfume of pink, white and lavender blossoms that made me want to drive at a more leisurely pace.

Maybe it was the sense of emptiness on campus. Instead of hurried students swarming along sidewalks and across streets, there was only an occasional walker, a random car parked curbside, seemingly ready to burst with the clothes and belongings that had filled someone's dorm room for nine months.

I returned an empty dish to an empty house that sits just about dead center of campus. Then, I sauntered home.

Ah, but quite soon I found myself picking up speed again. After all, it was May. College had let out for the summer, but everything else had not.

For those of us with school-age children, May runs a close second to December as the busiest month of the year. Parents cart their kids to choir concerts, band concerts, piano recitals, dance recitals, ball games, field days, gymnastics programs, awards programs, and graduations—not to mention school, which almost gets lost in the shuffle. All of life seems to be barreling toward that magic finish line when summer officially arrives and all schedules will cease.

This frantic push to the finish leaves us yearning for the day when we can lie back, catch our breath, and saunter instead of dash. Yet, when we finally burst across the threshold into summer, most of us will find that our vision of lazy, leisurely days was merely a mirage.

The current of yet another season will sweep us up and carry us along, and the difference won't be how fast we're moving but the direction we're heading. We'll find, not that we have no schedule, but that we have a new schedule. We'll find we have to run even to make time to play.

For some, this particular summer will bring a major life shift. Seniors will graduate. Engaged couples will marry. Families will move.

Even those who aren't facing such dramatic changes will have too much to do to sit on the front porch, fanning and drinking iced tea.

In every seasonal shift, we hurried Americans face the danger that we won't give ourselves time to process the change and, as a result, we'll end up running frantically down the wrong road. Yet, none of us has to dash headlong into a mid-summer nightmare.

A man named Joshua once faced a change of season. For 40 years, he'd served as assistant leader of a nation. Now the nation's leader was dead. Finding himself in charge, Joshua might have felt he had to hit the ground running in order to get his people where they needed to go.

Yet before heading out, Joshua did an amazing thing: He paused. He paused to give the people time to grieve for their former leader. He paused to listen to God.

When he did, God responded in an amazing way: He promised Joshua, *"I will be with you."* He challenged Joshua, *"Be strong and courageous" (Josh. 1:5,6 NIV).* He guided Joshua. In essence, God told him, "Pay careful attention to the words I've already written down. They'll keep you on track."

In the long shadows of lengthening days, let's pause to look ahead and get our bearings. Let's pause to look up and renew our strength.

Snapshot 51

□

Let's Just Stay

Water spurts upward to tree-top height, then rains back into the lake out of which it spurts. Manufactured homes with well-manicured yards stand amid tall pines and ever-green hardwoods. Temperatures hovering in the 70s welcome cloudless mornings, afternoon buildups, gentle breezes, lazy days.

For more than 15 years, my mother-in-law has lived in central Florida. Jerry, our girls, and I visit her once or twice a year. Some things have changed from visit to visit. When Megan and Amanda were younger, for example, I always went into the community pool with them. Later, I sat beside the pool while they swam. Now, they sunbathe by the pool, and I may or may not even go.

Other aspects of these getaway weeks have remained much the same. Each morning, we sleep an hour or two past the time the alarm at home would have roused us. We enjoy locally grown strawberries, tomatoes and grapefruits. Sitting with "Ginga" in her den, we listen while she chats freely about whatever's on her mind.

Most days, I spend 30 to 45 minutes walking through the quiet, shaded streets. I know none of the gray and white-haired people I pass, yet most of them speak. Some are sitting on porches, others are working in yards, still others are strolling or riding bicycles. Most make joking comments about how fast I'm walking.

Little do they know how far my thoughts and prayers are roaming. As I go, I'm evaluating the months since I've walked here last and asking God's direction for the days ahead. Before or after my walk, I'll sit with Bible in hand, absorbing words written thousands of years ago, yet still able to challenge and direct me today.

Ah, yes. Today. The sun plays hide-and-seek with scattered clouds while I lie reading a fiction book I'd never have time to read at home.

Around me, the swish of water mingles with the drone of voices and the cry of a bird.

Tomorrow, our latest stay in Florida will end. We'll fly home to resume our lives there. As soon as we step off the plane, we'll face the urgent clamor of schedules and responsibilities we've dared to neglect for most of a week.

At this moment, I identify with the apostle Peter, who once spent a getaway moment on a mountaintop with Jesus and surprise guests, Moses and Elijah. Reveling in the moment, Peter said (Deborah's paraphrase), "Let's just stay."

If Peter or I had hummed a few bars of Psalm 23, we'd have known better. That's the psalm that starts, *"The Lord is my shepherd, I shall not want."* The next sentence is the one I associate with our Florida trips: *"He makes me lie down in green pastures; He leads me beside quiet waters. He restores my soul."*

But in that psalm, notice what comes immediately after soul-restoring: *"He guides me in the paths of righteousness for His name's sake" (vv. 1–3 NASU).*

Resting places are vital. Most of us need more of them. But resting places are also strategic. True rest brings renewal. And genuine renewal doesn't leave us lazy and limp. It prepares us for returning.

So you see, I can't stay in my getaway place any more than Peter could stay on the mountain. Once restored, all who follow the shepherd have paths of righteousness to walk.

Snapshot 52

□

Happy Birthday

The following is an unpaid un-political announcement:
HAPPY BIRTHDAY!
Ah, yes, some of you have had birthdays recently. Others of you have not had a birthday in—oh, say, six or seven years. But most of you have this in common: You did not hear from me on the Big Day.

You may have sat by your phone, waiting. You may have run eagerly to the mailbox. You may have checked your e-mail on the hour—hoping for a gift, a greeting, anything to show I remembered and cared that you had reached yet another annual milestone.

No matter that some of you didn't want to be a year older. If you had to pass the mark anyway, you wanted me to celebrate.

Thing is, I did remember and I do care. It was the celebration part that fizzled. Somehow, these days, my time is not my own.

I'm well aware how lame that sounds. We all have 24 hours in a day. We all make choices about how we'll spend our time. If we'd just learn to "prioritize" and to "use our Daily Planners consistently," we'd have every one of our birthday cards bought, addressed and placed behind the appropriate monthly tab somewhere around January 3 each year.

So, okay, you didn't hear from me because I'm a sorry dog. And you didn't get a present because—well, do you remember the gifts I gave you in past years? No?

I didn't think so. A friend of mine has a knack for gift-giving. During one of our moves, when I was feverishly (but not very successfully) house-hunting, while also trying to acclimate to a new job and wondering when my family would ever be able to join me, this friend gave me a bottle of green stress-relief lotion.

Opening the package, I laughed out loud.

So why can't I—a relatively smart human being—come up with similarly wonderful gifts? All I know is: Great thought goes into my gift-giving. But you wouldn't know it by watching the faces of the recipients.

Oh, you're all quite gracious. And very polite. But time and again, I can tell I've missed the mark.

So this year (and last year, and maybe the year before that), I didn't shop. Which makes me a double louse.

The crushing weight of my louse-ness has been difficult to bear. It's awakened me at night, taunting, "You missed another one." It's goaded me by day, "Birthday basher!"

However, when I've tried to call or write you individually to rectify the situation, I haven't been able to connect: You weren't home. I'd misplaced your mailing address. The e-mail kept coming back.

Do you realize how humiliating it is when you can't even succeed at confessing?

In desperation, I'm giving it one more shot. (And if you never expected a birthday greeting from me at all, I'm speaking for all *your* relatives who've acted—or failed to act—in the same way as I.)

I love you. Please forgive me for not connecting with you on your special day. I let the obstacles defeat me.

In lieu of a gift you can't use or a birthday greeting that somebody made money for thinking up, would you accept a belated birthday blessing? People have been receiving this blessing ever since it was first written in an Old Testament book called (ironically): Numbers.

On your birthday and every day: *"The Lord bless you and keep you; the Lord make his face shine upon you and be gracious to you; the Lord turn his face toward you and give you peace" (Num. 6:24–26 NIV).*

Snapshot 53

□

Road Construction

Megan, Amanda, and I kept the highways hot one summer. Taking advantage of the school break to visit family and friends, we traveled through Indiana, Kentucky, Tennessee, Mississippi, Alabama, Illinois, and Missouri.

All along the way, we saw those flashing signs motorists most dread. The signs say: Road Construction Ahead. They mean: You're About to Be Very Frustrated.

The girls and I encountered these signs most often on interstates. In fact, after years of researching the matter, I've concluded that highway departments lay four-lane roads for one purpose—so they can close two of the lanes every summer to work on them.

Of course, four-lanes turned two-lanes make for even slower going than regular two-lane routes. For one thing, the speed limit drops from 65 miles an hour, not to 55, but to 45 or less. What's more, a yellow median barrier runs like a mole hill where the center line should be. Orange-and-white striped sticks all along the mole hill warn: Don't even think about trying to pass.

Unable to do otherwise, motorists follow in line—plodding, braking, and eagerly awaiting the place the road widens again. While our cars idle, our minds are racing, mentally calculating how far we could have driven by now if not for this delay.

Sometimes, the signs say how many miles the road construction will last. A good rule of thumb is: Don't believe them.

Traveling down one Mississippi highway, I read, "Road Construction Next 11 Miles." At *least* 11 l-o-n-g miles later, I passed a sign that said, "Resume normal speed." Just as I hit the resume button on the cruise control, I passed a third sign. It said, "Road Construction Next 26 Miles."

My husband Jerry, who is very practical (and who wasn't able to travel with the girls and me that summer because of his job), says road crews have to work in the summer to avoid the bad weather in the winter.

From his recliner, he sees the advantages the roadwork will yield in the long run. From my seat behind the steering wheel of our minivan, I see only the mess that's slowing me down today.

So why do I get the uncomfortable feeling that Jerry's perspective is the one I should adopt, not only when starting on a summer trip, but all along life's highway?

On life's path, God is constantly at work, renovating, not the road, but me. The process definitely causes delays. Many times, just when I think, "Good! That's done!" I run smack into another area the Lord is tearing up in order to redo.

While I'm fuming because I'm not where I think I should be at the moment, 2 Corinthians 4:17 reminds me, *"These troubles and sufferings of ours are, after all, quite small and won't last very long. Yet this short time of distress will result in God's richest blessing upon us forever and ever!" (TLB).*

Whether traveling or living, I need to learn to slow down and take the long look. Only then will I see beyond the barriers to the benefits.

Snapshot 54

□

O Say, Can You See?

Fifteen ladies sat looking at the papers and crayons in front of them, wondering if they'd accidentally entered a kindergarten room. Each paper held a coloring-book version of the American flag.

"Color the flag," I said. Dutifully, the women selected crayons and went to work. When finished, each showed a flag with red and white stripes and white stars on a blue background.

"Why did you choose those colors?" I asked.

"Because they're the colors of the American flag," they answered, laughing.

"How do you know?" I asked.

Duh. Those were the colors they'd been taught, the ones they had seen on American flags all their lives.

But what if someone decided to alter the colors of the American flag ever so slightly? What if that someone were a person of influence and so— while a few folks protested but most didn't even notice—other persons of influence followed suit?

What if these persons of influence were owners of flag-making companies and publishers of books with flag pictures and over time they continued to make subtle changes in the flag's colors? They made these changes deliberately because of their bent toward other colors. They made the changes slowly to bring along a general populace known to have a short memory.

By the time the colors were magenta, beige and turquoise, the influencers could silence the outcry of a few fanatics simply by saying, "All enlightened people know these are the correct and original colors of the American flag."

By the time the flag was black, pink and green, the masses were boo-ing and even jailing dissenters.

Then a few folks dared to search out actual documents from the flag creators. Finding that the American flag was supposed to be red, white and blue, they began to speak up. Few listened because everyone already had a flag and no one wanted to buy another one. Many never heard this startling news because it didn't suit the influencers to broadcast it.

And so, in this pretend story, the American people continued to fly flags that bore little resemblance to the one that inspired the Pledge of Allegiance and "The Star-Spangled Banner."

In real life, the American flag retains its original colors. But the details of our country's founding and the intent of our foundational documents have been subtly changed over time until the rulings in our courts and legislatures and the teachings in our history books bear little resemblance to anything our Founding Fathers would have recognized.

In particular, the Judeo-Christian ethic and the God who set its standards have been deleted and replaced with a plethora of gods, including humans themselves, and an ethic based on standards that fluctuate with the latest opinion poll.

Thousands of years before the American flag first flew, a king named Josiah came upon a document that clearly outlined the principles on which his nation had been founded. Reading the document, the king was shocked to learn how far he and his people had moved from those principles.

Ignoring every vestige of political correctness, King Josiah declared, *"God's anger must be burning furiously against us—our ancestors haven't obeyed a thing written in this book of God, followed none of the instructions directed to us" (2 Chr. 34:21 MSG).* Immediately, Josiah set to work to correct the situation.

If, indeed, we have much more at stake than color preference, might it be time for all of us to dig into the truth about our foundations as a nation? Might it be time to remember and return?

Note: Two excellent resources for this purpose are the book, *The Light and the Glory,* by Peter Marshall and David Manuel, and David Barton's website, www.wallbuilders.com.

Snapshot 55

□

Consult Elvis

Step back in time with me to August, 1997, the summer of the base-ball strike *and* the UPS strike. At the time, both were major calamities. In fact, the UPS strike was the biggest threat facing our nation—and maybe our world. That summer, I offered the following creative suggestion which, even today, might work for handling any problem of national importance:

Consult Elvis. Get him involved.

After all, the man in the White House is only the *President.* Elvis is the *King.* It doesn't matter that he's dead—that, in fact, we're approaching yet another anniversary of his untimely demise. Thanks to the miracle of electronic media, we have his image and his voice. Long live the King.

It also doesn't matter that Elvis himself never figured out how to handle power and money—that, in fact, he let them swallow him up. He could twist his body. Anyone with that capability ought to be able to man-age the twistings and turnings of corporate negotiations. Further, Elvis could croon. He could croon so that people would swoon, or scream, or cry, or throw things. Mostly, they would throw themselves at Elvis' feet.

In fact, they're still throwing themselves at Elvis' feet. If you don't believe me, go to Memphis and mingle among the more than 100,000 visi-tors supposed to gather to commemorate the anniversary of his death. Join one of the more than 500 active Elvis fan clubs. Better yet, join an Elvis church. According to a front-page article in the August 8, 1997, issue of *USA Today,* "Organized worship is one of countless offshoots of Elvis Pre-sley's mushrooming legacy."

If we call together the representatives of UPS and the Teamsters, put them in a room with an appropriate Elvis song (I'd suggest "Love Me Ten-der"), and pray to the larger-than-life-even-in-death image we've created, maybe the opposing sides will cry and fall into each other's arms. Then again, maybe they'll scream and throw things.

Like I said, it's only a suggestion.

Our second alternative, of course, is to call in the President. Actually, he's already been called. And who knows, by the time you read this, he may have ridden in like a knight on a white horse. However, at this point he has wisely chosen to refrain from action, knowing that presidential interference should come only when national health and safety are threatened, as in the case of the baseball strike.

This leaves us with a dilemma. We pray to Elvis, and find he's busy having an anniversary party. We pray to the President, and find he's busy planning the strategy best suited to political image-building. So to whom do we pray?

Many thinking people don't consider God an option. After all, he's invisible! Jesus came along before TV and film, so he didn't even leave us an image we can conjure up. Besides, this problem is big. It involves some really important people (as well as a whole lot of regular people). It involves money and power. It has global implications. I mean, we're not asking for help with homework, here.

What's more, if we really did seek God in this matter, he would expose all greed and deceit on both sides of the bargaining table. His solution would be fair and workable—but unacceptable, because it would require all of us to consider others more important than ourselves.

In this and other matters of national significance, I suppose we'll have to keep crying out to the King, or the President, or some other reasonable facsimile of deity.

After all, the Bible's an old book. It certainly isn't talking about us when it says, *"Claiming to be wise, they became fools and exchanged the glory of the immortal God for images resembling mortal man" (Rom. 1:22–23 HCSB).* Is it?

Snapshot 56

□

Brush with Reality

The day had gone rather well—until I dropped my daughters off for an activity. Needing to prepare for a presentation, I planned to drive to a nearby coffee shop, where I would sip and study.

On the way, I passed a drugstore. Well, no, I didn't pass it. I stopped in, intending to pick up a hair brush, then head on to my destination.

Once inside the store, I stood for some time before a confusing array of brushes. Finally, I chose a bargain, two brushes for the price of one.

On the way to check out, I passed the lipsticks. Well, no, I didn't pass them. I lingered in front of them. Talk about a confusing array. Numerous brands paraded before me, each having categories and subcategories of product in a profusion of shades.

I did need lipstick. In fact, the need almost bordered on emergency: My favorite tube was practically empty and the company had discontinued the shade. I quickly made the decision to purchase, then agonized over the choice.

At one point, an employee who had watched me systematically open the store's entire stock of samples, walked over and asked, "Can I help?" Finally, purchases in hand, I headed once again for my car.

I had turned onto the street when I realized how badly the wind had whipped my hair and how much it needed brushing. Irritated with myself for wasting too many minutes in the drugstore, I decided to brush and drive.

One hand on the wheel, eyes on the road, I fumbled in the bag for the brushes. Retrieving them, I tore at stubborn packaging. My frustration mounting, I managed to rip the brushes free from the wrapper—but not from each other. They were firmly bound together, back-to-back, by a thick plastic strip.

Okay, I decided, I'll use them hooked together.

On the first swoop through my hair, the brushes caught in my dangly silver earring. And there they both hung. I couldn't work them free. I couldn't let go of them for fear the weight would rip my ear. I couldn't get to the earring to unfasten it.

And so I drove down a well-lit street, holding two entangled brushes against my ear and refusing to glance at the car beside me. This car kept pace with my vehicle, not pulling ahead or lagging behind. I was convinced that, if I looked, I'd see people pointing my direction, doubled over in laughter.

When I pulled into a parking lot to extricate myself, my headlights revealed a lady getting into a nearby car. I saw her; she saw me. Hopefully, she thought the brushes were a new type cell phone.

By the time I reached the coffee shop, it was packed with others who had decided to sip and study. No seat remained. I ordered coffee, carried it out, drove back to the place where I'd dropped our daughters and sat in the car in the dark frantically trying to prepare my presentation.

You've heard of the principle of compounding interest? I had experienced the principle of compounding consequences. That is, a little deviation from the path can make you completely miss your destination.

That's not a big deal if you're on your own mission and it's a rather inconsequential one. But if you've started in a certain direction because you believe God wants you to go there, I urge you (from personal experience), follow the counsel of Deuteronomy 5:32: *"Be careful to do what the Lord your God has commanded you; do not turn aside to the right or to the left"* *(NIV)*.

Snapshot 57

□

Miracle of the Locust

It wasn't your regular garden variety of miracle. Or maybe it was.

I'd flown to Kansas to speak at a women's retreat. Actually, after I deplaned in Tulsa, Oklahoma, my hostess drove me two hours north into southeast Kansas. Along the way, we passed flat terrain, wheat fields and occasional mountains of gravel called "chat piles."

Stepping from the car, I realized that Kansas was having a heat wave, and we were going to get the full impact of it. The retreat center consisted of a few rather dilapidated cabins, a dining hall cooled only by two large, standing fans, and the "tabernacle," where I would be speaking.

The tabernacle had a roof with fluorescent lights and ceiling fans hanging from it. Other than a few supporting beams, it had no walls. A stage area at the front had a faulty board right behind the speaker's stand. Wooden benches with no backs stood ready to welcome retreat-goers.

After supper, ladies who had braved the heat found seats on the wooden benches. Waiting my turn to speak, I wondered if anyone would be able to understand what I said over the locusts chirping in chorus all around us. I wondered who could concentrate with so much to distract. Discouraged, I thought, *It's going to be almost impossible for us to hear from God in this setting.*

Then, perspiring, I stood at the podium. The floor squeaked and gave. The locusts cried in chorus. The ladies fanned.

Asking everyone to bow their heads, I prayed aloud. The suffocating distraction remained. Instead of launching into my talk, I asked the women to pray silently, talking to God about anything that was burdening them. A few moments later, I asked them to pray silently for anyone attending the retreat whom they knew was worried or hurting. Finally, I asked if anyone had a prayer request they would mention aloud.

One by one, women named requests. One by one, we prayed for each.

That was when one determined locust discovered the fluorescent light. With vigor, he would hurl himself into it, buzz violently, drop away, then attack again. The noise all but drowned out my words.

After the prayer, I began to speak, and the locust quieted down, apparently finding other places to flit. But then, just as I reached a crucial part of my talk—the part I believed God especially wanted us all to hear and obey—the locust renewed his attacks on the light.

After about the third loud buzz, at the moment he was dropping away from the light fixture, I heard myself stop in mid-sentence of my talk and speak one word directly to that insect. "Die!" I exclaimed.

The locust fell to the ground and lay there.

All of us stared at him. He didn't move. "If he really dies, I'll probably faint," I joked. Still, the locust lay on his back on the concrete floor. "Of course, he may have just decided to take a nap," I quipped. The ladies laughed. I resumed my talk.

At that point, all of us seemed to forget the heat, the discomfort and the night noises around us. We all sensed that God had come to the tabernacle. I was the mouthpiece, but he was delivering the message. No one wanted to miss it, least of all me.

At the end of my talk, we all stood in a large circle, joining hands. Just before we closed in prayer, the lady standing next to me nudged me. "Deborah, look," she said.

The locust lay where he had fallen, dead.

Snapshot 58

◻

Seeking Shade

It's a little out of place. The white two-story farmhouse, with the ramshackle red barn behind it and the lofty trees around it, should overlook acres of fields. Until recently, it did overlook acres of fields where corn and soybeans grew.

Now, the farmhouse sits at the entrance to a neighborhood of brick-and-siding homes, still popping up and built as close together as lot lines will allow. Because of their former cornfield status, few of the lots have trees, except the just-planted kind that, as yet, offer little in the way of beauty or shade.

Our own yard bears only a lonely spruce, not yet as tall as me. We purchased it live and used it as a Christmas tree our first December in Indiana. After the holidays, Jerry planted it in a hole he managed to dig in the frozen ground. To our amazement, the spruce lived. The pin oak we planted last summer did not. Since we continue to find other needs more pressing than buying gawky trees with only the distant promise of stateliness, our flat rectangle of a yard remains nearly tree free.

When thunderstorms, tornado warnings, and ice hit our area, I'm glad we don't have tall trees creaking and cracking overhead. When leaf-raking season rolls around, I'm content with our treeless state. Today, though, I miss my yard with trees.

Maybe it's because I feel a little out of place and a lot out of sync with the world. Maybe it's because too many disappointments have hit too close together. Today, I need to stand in the shadow of something taller than me—something sturdy and living, deep-rooted and lasting, that whispers timeless secrets as the wind passes through.

Instead, I sit, gazing out my home-office window, past one small lot that hasn't yet sold, toward the trees in the farmhouse yard. At the forefront of my view, a weeping willow spreads its branches beside the red barn. The willow stands near the border between yard and vacant lot, reigning over both like a monarch with royal robes flowing.

Season after season, I love watching that willow. Usually, it provides me all the "tree fix" I need. In fact, if it were possible, I'd buy the lot that keeps that tree in my view, just to prevent anyone from building on it.

But today, I realize that *gazing* isn't the same as "sitting in the shade of." The willow stands on property belonging to the farmhouse owners. If I were to sit under it, I'd be trespassing.

Of course, I could go to a nearby park and enjoy the trees there. But a poet and a prophet offer me another solution.

In Psalm 121:5, the poet declares, *"The Lord himself watches over you! The Lord stands beside you as your protective shade"* (NLT). In Isaiah 25:4, the prophet says, to God, *"You have been a refuge for the poor, a refuge for the needy in his distress, a shelter from the storm and a shade from the heat"* (NIV).

Seeking shade, it's to this God I go—a bit reluctantly, a bit awkwardly. I'm no stranger to him, nor he to me. But I stomped away a day or two ago, angry he hasn't done more to protect my family from hurts that keep getting worse instead of better.

Facing him again, I know it's time to stand in the shadow of someone bigger than me—someone sturdy and living, deep-rooted and lasting, who whispers timeless secrets as his spirit-breath sweeps through.

Snapshot 59

□

Butterfly Days

Tell me, have you seen them? Every September, little yellow butterflies are out and about in northeast Mississippi. Back in 1977—can it be that long ago?—I first noticed them dancing on the September air. I was dancing on air, too, as the 17th rolled around. It was my wedding day.

It was Jerry's wedding day, too. And I'm sure he would have been dancing along with me, if he hadn't been trying so hard not to faint. I had asked him to quote aloud one verse of Scripture as part of the ceremony. He had agreed, even though he was far from convinced that his memory would function in that particular setting.

Walking the aisle of our church in Corinth, Mississippi, holding lightly to my father's arm and looking into Jerry's white face (that seemed especially colorless in contrast to his beige tuxedo), I wasn't so sure he could do it, either. But his voice was strong as he spoke these words from Hosea 2:19: *"I will betroth you to Me in righteousness . . . and in compassion, and I will betroth you to Me in faithfulness" (NASB).*

Jerry had asked me to sing a song. I was convinced I could do that. Up until the moment I opened my mouth to sing, I was convinced I could do it. However, I had greatly underestimated my own nervousness and the quivering it would produce in my voice. Somehow, I made it all the way through what seemed like endless verses of "We Are One in the Bond of Love." Those who were moved to tears were not crying over the melodic beauty. To any of you who were there, I apologize for putting you through that.

A decade later, yellow butterflies were flitting again when our second daughter arrived. Amanda showed up on our tenth wedding anniversary. Although we were living in Corinth at the time, she was born in a Memphis hospital. During the delivery, Jerry's face was about as pale as it had been at the wedding. The difference was: he wore blue scrubs, and I didn't try to sing.

That night, he and my parents celebrated by going out to a local restaurant to eat. I should have known then that anniversaries were going to take a back seat to birthday parties in the years ahead.

In September, 1997, Amanda had been planning her tenth-birthday party for weeks. She wanted to have Mexican refreshments and American Girl games. I was so busy helping her with her plans that it didn't occur to me until the week of her birthday that the anniversary we would celebrate that same day was our twentieth.

We have friends who celebrated their twentieth anniversary by taking a trip to Canada. We're already past our 25th now—and still haven't taken an anniversary trip. Since 1994, we haven't even been able to admire yellow butterflies in September because we've flitted away to live far from northeast Mississippi.

But, hey, don't you go feeling sorry for us. Trips come and go, as do anniversaries, but daughters are definitely keepers. So are husbands who live out their promises of love and faithfulness.

Before our wedding, I wrote a sort of prose poem that includes a prayer I'm still praying. Built on the idea that our marriage created a union as fresh and alive as a butterfly, the piece ended this way:

"We're new. We can fly. God grant that we won't pass our days on the ground. Let us always be found lifted up by your power, enabled each moment, each hour, to show forth our Lord in our lives, in our marriage… Yellow butterfly days are here."

I'm happy to report: They're still here all these years later—whether we can see the little critters or not. For, though I won't try to sing it, Jerry and I are one in the bond of love.

Snapshot 60

□

The Caramel Controversy

Apple season set me up. Our neighbor brought us a bag of apples from her home state of Pennsylvania right after I'd bought locally grown apples at the grocery store. Surveying all that red-skinned fruit, our daughters cried in unison: "Please get some caramel dip."

I complied, and they promptly began taking apples and caramel dip in their school lunches.

Let me pause here to take a survey: When you say the word *caramel,* do you say "CARE-uh-mul" or "CAR-mul"? My family says "CARE-uh-mul." But one of our daughters quickly learned that everyone else in her class says "CAR-mul."

When we moved from Mississippi to Indiana, we took our pronunciation with us. It had served us well for many years, and we planned to continue using it. Ah, but my daughter's classmates could not get over the wondrous (and thoroughly amusing) way she said their word.

My daughter protested to her teacher that a word spelled c-a-r-a-m-e-l should be pronounced the three-syllable way. This teacher, who likes to tease, and who shall remain nameless because I am compassionate and because I want my daughter to complete elementary school, replied, "Well, I guess if you've grown up around enough hillbillies, you can say CARE-uh-mul."

My daughter, who knows her teacher likes to tease, came home laughing about the remark. Her hillbilly mama felt somewhat like blacks must feel when someone calls them the "n" word. I certainly don't mind anyone associating me with hills. I'm a product, not of the endlessly flat Mississippi delta, but of the hilly northeast corner of the state.

In fact, the May my husband went to Muncie, Indiana, for a job interview and called home to tell me he'd been offered the job, the first question I asked had nothing to do with people or living conditions or schools. It had everything to do with terrain. "Is it flat?" I asked.

"Yes," he answered solemnly.

But guess what? We moved anyway. And we liked east central Indiana (although now that we had snow in winter, we had to look to find a hill to sled down).

What I do mind is someone linking me with a term that makes me sound inferior. So, I promptly did what every self-respecting hillbilly would have done in my situation. I marched to the dictionary and looked up the word *caramel*. Do you want to know the preferred pronunciation, according *The American Heritage Dictionary, Second College Edition?* CARE-uh-mul. (For you who are disappointed, CAR-mul is also acceptable.)

I wanted to photocopy the page and send it back to the teacher, along with a note saying: "Sometimes hillbillies are right." But I didn't. As one Old Testament proverb says, *"A man's wisdom gives him patience; it is to his glory to overlook an offense" (Prov. 19:11 NIV).* I'm just sure that verse applies to women, too.

And it doesn't just apply during apple season. In every season of life, offense is something we're way too quick both to give and to take. Instead of enjoying our differences and realizing how dull things would be without them, we tend to view life as an "us" against "them" battle. As a matter of course, we belittle others or assume they're belittling us.

Yet Romans 14 urges all of us—regardless how we say caramel or what color our skin is or where we grew up: *"Let us pursue the things which make for peace and the building up of one another" (v. 19 NASB).*

Snapshot 61

□

Search for Brown November

Excuse me, but has anyone seen November? I know I'm dating myself, but I do seem to recall a time when it came right after October. Now, of course, December starts before Halloween.

I realize that, to most people, November's not good for much. The World Series is over, and the Superbowl won't trot around again until next year. The days are growing shorter; the nights longer. Generally, fall foliage has passed peak, and real snow hasn't arrived. Looking around, we see mostly shades of gray and brown.

Of course, some people do have November birthdays. That's important, especially to them. And near the end of the month, we do get a brief holiday. Some still call it Thanksgiving, but a more appropriate name might be Eating Too Much and Watching Football. The grocers, turkey suppliers, and football franchises are about the only ones who make a profit from it.

Except that the extra time off provides us a grand opportunity—for early Christmas shopping. It is hoped, of course, that we'll set our minds on Christmas shopping long before this brief, but strategically timed, November holiday. It is hoped that, from the minute we turn off the porch light on October 31, we'll spend every waking moment planning for and making purchases to put under someone's tree.

One year, the day my calendar said November 1, we received no less than five Christmas catalogs in our mail. And that was just the beginning. From Christmas displays to "pre-holiday sales" to preparations for Christmas musicals, everything except my calendar shouted, "DECEMBER."

Three days after the catalogs arrived, one of our elementary-age daughters remarked, "This year's gone so fast."

"We still have two months," I reminded her.

"It doesn't seem like it," she said. With November just beginning, even children seem to feel, not only that December's already arrived, but that it's practically over.

Now don't get me wrong. I like December. I enjoy Christmas. But, call me quirky, I think we ought to leave room for November, too. Yes, it's brown and gray. Yes, it's practically profitless. But that's okay. We don't have to dress this month in a Santa costume in order for it to have value.

Ecclesiastes 3:1 says, *"There is a time for everything, and a season for every activity under heaven" (NIV)*. Verse 11 insists that God *"has made everything beautiful in its time."*

In November, grown-ups can rake leaves, and children can scatter them. Friends can sit together, savoring a good conversation, a hot cup of coffee, spiced tea or cider—and maybe even a warm fire. A person can throw on a jacket and take a brisk walk, or find a cozy chair and travel by book wherever her heart desires.

In November, we can give heartfelt thanks for our country's godly heritage and God's present, undeserved blessings. We can work and play, laugh and cry. We can reflect on life and eternity. We can make the most of the time—or hurry past it.

Most likely, none of us would choose brown and gray all year long. But if we don't stop to appreciate what God has made beautiful in this time, we may get all our presents and miss all our moments.

Snapshot 62

□

Squanto

If you've ever faced hardships, you may want to hear this story. It's an amazing story. In fact, if I wrote it into a novel, you'd say it was too coincidental, too far-fetched. But because it really happened, it may help you see that far-fetched and wonderful things can come from hardships. It may even, possibly, provoke you to give thanks.

It all started 400 years ago when a Native American named Squanto lived near Cape Cod with his tribe, the Patuxets. One day, an English sea captain kidnapped Squanto and four other Patuxets, carted them off to England, taught them English and pumped them for information about the New World. Nine years passed before Squanto linked up with a second sea captain, who took him back across the Atlantic to his home.

As soon as Squanto stepped off that ship, the captain of another vessel invited him and 19 other Patuxets aboard. The captain pretended to want to barter but really wanted a cargo of slaves. This captain took his captives *back* across the Atlantic to Spain, where Squanto was bought and freed by friars, who introduced him to the Christian faith.

Are you still following here? I told you this would seem far-fetched.

As soon as he could secure passage, Squanto left Spain for England. More time passed before he again sailed for home. In spring of 1620, 15 years after he was first abducted, Squanto stepped ashore at what we now know as Plymouth, Massachusetts. There, he found no one at all from his tribe. Two years after his second kidnapping, a plague had killed every man, woman, and child among his people.

Of all that had befallen him, this blow was by far the worst. In despair, Squanto wandered into the camp of another tribe, the Wampanoags. He remained with them for a year, utterly desolate.

Meanwhile, a little group of Pilgrims landed in the New World and

137

settled at Plymouth, on land that had formerly belonged to the Patuxets but now belonged to no one. That first winter, nearly half the Pilgrims died.

The future looked bleak for the 55 survivors (17 of whom were children). They had little food and only English wheat and barley to plant. In March, the grieving man who had twice been abducted by Englishmen heard about the little colony and went calling. Instead of single-handedly wiping them out, he single-handedly saved them. Before the next winter, he had taught the Pilgrims what they needed to know to survive in the Massachusetts wilderness, and they had embraced him as their own.

In October, the Pilgrim governor declared a day of Thanksgiving. Pilgrims and Indians celebrated together. Whom did Squanto and his new-found family thank? The God the Phillips New Testament calls *"the blessed controller of all things" (1 Tim. 6:15).*

Why did they thank him? He certainly hadn't kept them from hardship. But he'd done something even more amazing. Romans 8:28 describes it this way: *"Moreover we know that to those who love God, who are called according to his plan, everything that happens fits into a pattern for good" (Phillips).*

Through his trials, Squanto learned English, came to know Christ, survived the plague that obliterated his tribe and returned to New England six months before the arrival of the Pilgrims. The Pilgrims, who were supposed to settle 100 miles south, chose instead the one place where help awaited them.

Which, then, is more far-fetched: to attribute it all to coincidence, or to give thanks to the God who—no matter how vast the wilderness—can bring together a man desperately needing purpose and a people desperately needing life?

Snapshot 63

□

The Tent

The tent went up the same week I found out Daddy needed heart surgery. It was a day when rain alternately poured and drizzled, keeping our two daughters indoors. Our younger daughter, Amanda, erected the tent in our living room.

She started with a large fitted sheet and four dining room chairs. Placing the chairs several feet apart and facing outward, she draped the corners of the sheet over the chair backs. This created a canopy with plenty of room underneath. Next, Amanda hung assorted lightweight blankets from the sheet to the floor, forming the tent flaps. She used heavier blankets to cover the chairs, incorporating them into the tent walls.

In the cubbyhole underneath each chair, she neatly arranged carefully chosen stuff—books in one, Beany Babies in another, bed clothes and hairbrush in the third, art supplies in the fourth. Across the floor of her tent, she laid out a sleeping bag and pillows. I added a small reading lamp to the décor, advising her to use it only when one or more of the "flaps" were open.

For two nights, Amanda slept in her tent. Then, deciding her bed was softer, she rearranged her tent furniture. The chairs, fitted sheet, blankets and cubbyholes all stayed; but after removing the sleeping bag, she placed a sofa cushion in the middle of the tent floor to make a low table. On the table, she placed a computer game. Around the table, she arranged three "seats," a folded sleeping bag and two folded blankets.

For most of the week, she's dressed in the tent, read in the tent, played in the tent. I know her hideaway can't stay forever, eating up our entire living room. But as of this writing, I haven't had the heart to tell her to take it down.

In the not-so-distant past, Amanda made tents with her older sister, Megan. Together, they played in them for hours on end. Now that Megan's middle-school age, she passes the tent by without any inclination to climb inside.

Not far behind her sister in age, Amanda may not have an interest in draping sheets and blankets over chairs very much longer. Maybe it's knowing this tent could be our last that makes me want to leave it up.

Maybe it's knowing how quickly life changes that makes me want to climb inside, pull down the flaps, and hide away for awhile.

Of course, I can't make life's changes go away by trying to ignore them. Our girls will continue to grow. Daddy will have open-heart surgery. I want to be there for both.

Still, the idea of a hideaway draws me.

In Old Testament days, God met with his people in a tent. He did that, in part, because tents are portable. Wherever his people went, he was there, available. Yet, they had to make an effort to approach him, to draw aside to meet with him.

Once, when a poet-king named David felt overwhelmed by life's shifts, he told God, *"I long to dwell in your tent forever" (Psalm 61:4 NIV)*. David could have relied on his own resources to handle life's changes; but instead, withdrawing from the hubbub, he gained fresh strength and perspective from the unchanging one.

I can identify with David's longing. And like him, I don't have to crawl into a shelter made of sheets, blankets and chairs to fulfill that longing. Wherever I go, whatever life brings, God is there, available. Every time I choose to approach him, every time I draw aside to meet him, he welcomes me into his tent.

Snapshot 64

☐

Heart Check

He went in for a regular checkup and found his heart had deceived him. He hadn't experienced pain or numbness; but when he mounted the treadmill, his EKG showed something irregular. The next day, catheterization revealed blockages in three arteries that supply blood to the heart. Two of the three were 95 percent clogged.

His doctor called the condition "the silent killer." In some cases, the doctor said, this type heart disease produces no symptoms. As a result, the people suffering from it don't know anything is wrong until a major heart attack hits, or (as in my daddy's case) until a heart check reveals the problem.

On a Monday, four days after he walked, unsuspecting, into his doctor's office, Daddy underwent triple bypass surgery. The night before the surgery, he and Mama sat around their kitchen table chatting with all four of their adult children, a son-in-law, a daughter-in-law and three of their eight grandchildren. (We had dropped in from such places as Arizona, Florida, Indiana and down the street.) In the spirit of the light-hearted banter floating around that table, my brother Jim suggested an alternative to the surgery: Drano. "It's tough on the clogs, but won't hurt the pipes," Jim quipped.

The next morning, we gathered around another table. This time, Daddy was lying on it. As the medical personnel came to wheel him into the operating room, Daddy said, "You know, that Drano may not have been such a bad idea."

He repeated the same thing a time or two after the surgery, while still lying in the critical care unit, hooked to all manner of tubes and monitors.

In the days immediately after the surgery, doctors kept telling us Daddy was doing well. But doing well and feeling well are two different things. During those days, Daddy didn't feel nearly as perky as he did before people went to tinkering with his chest.

Yet for all his remarks to the contrary, he knew Drano wasn't the answer. Nor was the answer to ignore a problem his heart told him did not exist.

The Sunday morning before the Monday surgery, a guest preacher at my parents' church used Jeremiah 17:9–10 as his sermon text. Daddy looked rather wry when the preacher read, *"The heart is more deceitful than all else and is desperately sick; who can understand it? I, the Lord, search the heart . . ." (NASU).*

Sitting beside Daddy in that pew, I realized what a wise and difficult thing my father was doing. His heart was saying, "I feel fine. No problem. Surgery will just mean useless trauma."

In order to go through what he did, Daddy had to believe the physicians who searched his heart and recognized the deceit in it. Eight years later, still in good health, he's delighted that he did.

But during the week of Daddy's surgery, while sitting in that church pew and later in the hospital waiting room, I contemplated the millions who are walking around with a desperately sick heart still deceiving them. Their problem lies, not with the physical heart, but with the heart in the sense that Jeremiah meant it—the control center of their lives.

These people think they're okay. Symptom-free, they're confident it won't hurt to keep living as they're living. They haven't accepted the diagnosis of the God who's already done a heart check on us all. With every heartbeat, sin intrudes a little further into critical places in their lives. They may joke about it. But they've never let the Great Physician do the major surgery required to correct it.

Unaware or unheeding, they're harboring the silent killer.

Snapshot 65

□

How?

I think I understand *why* he started, but can't begin to fathom *how* he finished.

How did he stay in a garden, of all places, with even his closest followers sleeping, while he agonized under pressure so intense that he perspired blood? How did he keep from walking off into the darkness?

With new life budding all around him, how did he pronounce his own death sentence? Later, an angry mob and an appeasing government would presumably impose the sentence. But he knew his death had been decreed by the father who loved him. How did he say again and again, "I want your will, not mine"?

How did he take charge when perhaps 600 trained and armed soldiers stormed his place of retreat to arrest him? How did he knock them all to the ground with the words, "I am"?

How did he interrogate Pilate, the Roman governor charged with interrogating him?

How did he remain silent when falsely accused? How did he remain still when taunted and spat upon? How did he keep from zapping them all to demonstrate that his claims weren't heresy, but truth?

How did he live through the flogging that tore every piece of flesh from his back? Afterward, how did he stand at all, much less walk? Beaten beyond recognition, how did he carry a wooden crossbeam to the place of his own execution?

How did he keep from dying before his mission was accomplished? How did he cling to life when, able to lie down at last, he was nailed hand and foot to that beam? Raised above the heads of those who hated him, those who grieved for him and those who liked the show, how was he able to breathe?

Breathing required pushing up on those pierced feet. Breathing required ramming splintered wood into his shredded back. Breathing required an unfathomable commitment to finish.

How did he speak even once, much less seven times? How did he express compassion and forgiveness toward others—instead of angry curses?

Earlier, he'd said, *"The Father and I are one" (John 10:30 TEV)*. To separate "one," you must rip it apart. When that awful ripping happened, how was he able to cry, *"My God, my God, why have you forsaken me?" (Matt. 27:46 NLT)*.

Repeating the opening words of Psalm 22, he carried us to an entire song that foretold his agony beyond what he could utter.

In only a few documented cases, people have been declared medically dead—only to resume breathing. But the followers who deserted their leader in the garden, the guys who hid in an upstairs room while he died, came out of that room declaring that the man Jesus had not just backed out of death temporarily but rather had broken through it permanently, opening the way for all who would to follow. Those formerly certified cowards would not—could not—change their story, even when faced with exile, torture and death.

So how did this dead leader live?

The *why,* by the way, has to do with his outrageous love for all people, none of whom by God's standards is basically good. Ah, but the *how* is linked with the other essential in the equation: holiness.

Romans 1 calls him *"our Lord Jesus Christ,"* describing him this way: *"as to his humanity, he was born a descendant of David; as to his divine holiness, he was shown with great power to be the Son of God by being raised from death" (vv. 3–4 TEV)*.

Did Jesus finish his impossible assignment because he alone is basically God?

Each of us faces the impossible assignment of overcoming evil (especially our own evil) with good. Could Jesus alone be the *how?*

Snapshot 66

□

Remote Connection

One night our phone rang. It was the land line—only without the "line." Yes, some years before, we'd gone portable.

So, anyway, the phone rang. It was obviously close at hand. But the exact location was anybody's guess. (Phones that can be carried wherever you like can also be deposited in the oddest of places.)

Amanda and I were sitting on the couch, watching TV, when the ringing began. Dutifully, I reached for what looked like the portable phone, picked it up and turned it over.

Beware of TV remotes disguised as portable phones! You can answer them all day, but alas, to no avail.

Rushing to my defense, let me say that I did not actually speak into the TV remote. I didn't even push one of the 243 buttons on the remote in hopes of answering the call. Yes, the combination of nearby ring and similar-looking backsides fooled me temporarily. But one glance at the front of the remote revealed the error of my ways.

Eventually, I did find the actual phone, but by then Amanda and I were laughing so hard I had trouble saying hello.

All of which reminds me of Joshua, though I don't exactly know why. Joshua never had a portable phone, nor a TV remote. He'd just been appointed leader of a nation, with the impossible assignment of following Moses, a man who had led long and exceptionally well.

On the day Joshua needed to step out and begin leading, God spoke to him. God's words, recorded in Joshua 1, include the following: *"This book of instruction must not depart from your mouth; you are to recite it day and night, so that you may carefully observe everything written in it. For then you will prosper and succeed in whatever you do"* (vv. 8–9 HCSB).

The "book of instruction" to which God referred is a compilation of five volumes that Joshua's predecessor had written down. They're still in existence and are included as the first five books in the Bible. Moses, the writer, insisted God had told him what to write. Joshua too believed the words were from God.

This "book," and indeed all the Bible, instructs us in how to live successfully.

In his new role, Joshua would surely get lots of advice from well-meaning people. He would have lots of ideas of his own. How would he know which ideas were on target and which were off the wall?

Maybe this is where the TV remote comes in.

You see, I'm well acquainted with phones, having talked on them all my life. Joshua was to be well acquainted with God's instructions, to recite them and obey them all his life. In attempting to answer a call, I made a silly goof. Yet, because of my familiarity with phones, I caught myself quickly. In attempting to lead a nation, Joshua would make some silly goofs. Yet, because of his familiarity with God's words, he would be able to catch himself quickly. As he obeyed, he would succeed and prosper.

When it comes to prosperity and success, lots of people today hear the ring—but they're trying to answer TV remotes and don't even know it.

Psalm 19 says, *"The instruction of the Lord is perfect, reviving the soul."* What's more, *"there is great reward in keeping"* God's words *(vv. 7,11 HCSB)*. Yet how often do we ignore the call to true abundance while busily pushing buttons we're just sure will connect us with the answer? That's not laughable. It's tragic.

Whether you're seeking telephones or success, you can't be tricked for long when you know the real thing.

Snapshot 67

□

Silent Fear

"I have silent fear," 10-year-old Amanda said matter-of-factly.

We were discussing bees and wasps and a camping trip our older daughter Megan wanted to take. Because Megan has been known to go ballistic at the sight of a flying, buzzing insect, Jerry had reminded her that "nature" includes bugs.

Megan was insisting she had outgrown such childish hysteria when Amanda joined the conversation. "Megan screams and cries and runs," she said. "I get afraid of things too, but I don't show it. I have silent fear."

While the conversation moved ahead around me, I sat pondering our younger daughter's depth of insight and her likeness to her mama. At 10, she'd pinpointed what I'd experienced ever since I could remember but hadn't identified until after rounding 40.

When I was young, my two sisters and I would pile into the car with Daddy each weekday morning for the drive to school. Mama stood at the door with our little brother Jim to wave 'bye. Those days, cars didn't start so well on cold mornings. At least, ours didn't.

Daddy would crank. The car would die. Daddy would crank. The car would die. About the third time the car spluttered, my youngest sister Judy would dive out the car door, crying and yelling, "It's going to explode! The car's going to explode!"

Daddy and Mama tried to reassure her, "Judy, the car's not going to explode."

I don't think they convinced her. As I remember it, she stood outside the car (a much safer place than in it) until the motor decided to cooperate.

My family members still tease Judy about her morning leaps from the back seat of a cold car. But what they don't know (or didn't until now) is that one daughter who sat calmly in the vehicle during Daddy's fruitless attempts to crank it felt the same stark terror as the daughter who jumped out.

Because I didn't want to show my fear, I managed to keep my seat. Still, I didn't conquer the fear. I simply hid it.

Over the years, I've struggled with silent fear whenever I've faced great change: upcoming marriage, my first pregnancy, a trip to the Soviet Union, our move from Mississippi to Indiana.

When we moved again (this time, to Oklahoma), one fear in particular kept clutching at my throat: In a market flooded with homes due to the closing of four major factories, I was terrified that our house would sit unsold forever, draining our resources and preventing us from being able to buy a home in Oklahoma.

A silly fear? Maybe. But there were houses down the block from us that had sat unsold for nearly a year.

The day after our family discussion about bees and camping and fear, we worshiped in a little church near Indianapolis. Purple banners with gold lettering hung at different places around the sanctuary. Each banner contained Hebrew writing and, below it, an English translation.

As the preacher talked, my eyes kept traveling beyond him to the banner on the front wall. It offered a rather unique rendering of a name Abraham called God in Genesis 22. It declared, *"Yehovah's Provision Will Be Seen."*

The more I pondered that banner, the more I felt it was God's silent answer to my silent fear.

Interestingly, after we moved to Oklahoma, our Indiana house did sit unsold for several months. But during that time, we miraculously managed payments on two houses.

Since then, whenever I've sensed fear stalking me, I've turned to face it, crying, "The Lord's provision will be seen." Time and again, I've watched the truth frighten fear away.

Snapshot 68

□

Dry, Weary Land

I didn't think the heat would be a problem. True, we had moved to Oklahoma City from Indiana just at the start of summer. Until four years earlier, however, I'd always lived in the South. Mostly, I'd lived in northeast Mississippi, where summer heat is a fact of life.

But from mid-June to mid-September of that year, the heat in central Oklahoma was relentless; the rain, nonexistent. Ranchers sold off their cattle, knowing they had no way of feeding them. Crops died in the seed. Day after day, temperatures topped 100. Morning after morning, the wide blue sky looked down on brittle-white grass, dead bushes, dying trees, wilting buildings.

People kept telling me, "This isn't normal." Normal or not, it wasn't fun.

One week that August, I spent two days in the Oklahoma panhandle with seven other women. None of us were prepared for what we found there.

Supposedly, the panhandle is the arid part of the state. Weary of dead vegetation, we were expecting anything but a scenic trip.

Sure enough, the landscape was depressing as we set out heading northwest from Oklahoma City. But about three hours into our trip—about the time we should have encountered desert—we began to encounter—life. Green fields, soft grasses, yellow and white wildflowers delighted and invited us. We oohed. We aahed. We threatened to stop the car and pick the flowers.

True, the creeks over which we passed had no water. And the green in the grasses was light and tentative, not the deep hue of a lush land.

But like a sip of cool water, what we saw made us ever so thirsty for more.

On the return trip, clouds formed. One cloud moved overhead, slinging heavy raindrops onto the fields, the roadway, the windshield. We wanted to jump out of the car and play. We wanted to lasso the cloud and bring it home with us, like a kite in tow.

During that shower, an old hymn came to my mind, its words expressing a prayer from my heart for all of us living in the parched places: "Pass me not, O gentle Savior. Hear my humble cry. While on others Thou art calling, Do not pass me by."

On the heels of the hymn, I remembered part of a line from a much older song. It said something about "a dry and weary land where there is no water."

Later, I located the line in Psalm 63, a poem-song written in a desert. David, the composer, knew how it felt to live in a place of drought. Like us, he had sagged under the oppressive heat of a parched land. Like us, he had thirsted for relief. But amazingly, he didn't cry for rain.

He said, *"O God, you are my God, earnestly I seek you; my soul thirsts for you, my body longs for you, in a dry and weary land where there is no water" (v. 1 NIV)*.

Oklahoma isn't the only place that's suffered drought lately. In a very real way, our whole nation can be described as "a dry and weary land." Day after day, the sun rises into a cloudless sky. But instead of welcoming the sun, we find ourselves trying to hide from its scorching heat. People, families, churches, and communities are parched, lethargic, spent. We long for a good, slow, soaking shower.

Yet David has reminded me that the dry times can be profitable times if they produce in us a deep, unrelenting thirst for God.

Snapshot 69

□

Microscopic Faith

A motley group of men faced a staggering task. Before them stood a father, begging them to stop the seizures that threatened his son's life. None of the men were doctors. None were religious leaders. They knew about taxes and fishing and the like. Not healing.

At least, they hadn't known anything about healing until they'd met a man who had the power to heal. He seemed to do it effortlessly. He did it everywhere he went. His name was Jesus.

After these men followed Jesus around for awhile, listening to what he said, watching what he did, he called them aside and did something we might wish someone would do for us: He *"gave them authority to drive out evil spirits and to heal every disease and sickness" (Matt. 10:1 NIV).*

The day the man brought his son for healing, Jesus' followers tried to do what he'd given them authority to do. They tried to heal that boy. Didn't work.

Then Jesus walked up. He listened to the story, identified the root problem (in this case, demon possession), and performed the healing quicker than you or I could blink. Afterward, he told his followers why their efforts hadn't yielded any results. "Because you have so little faith," he said.

By "so little," he must have meant "microscopic," because he went on to say, *"I tell you the truth, if you have faith as small as a mustard seed, you can say to this mountain, 'Move from here to there' and it will move. Nothing will be impossible for you" (Matt. 17:20 NIV).*

I tested that statement once. It was the summer after my freshman year in high school. Several of my friends and I were attending a summer conference in the mountains of North Carolina. The first morning out, as we hiked from our lodge to the cafeteria, we took a turn in the path and saw, rising before us, a mountain.

It was an "ooh-ah" moment. The mountain loomed, imposing,

unmoving. We stopped to admire, before continuing our trek. After the "oohs and ahs," one of us remembered the promise about mustard-seed faith, and, half-joking, we determined we had the faith needed to move that mountain.

The next morning, we took the same turn in the path—and stood gaping. The mountain was gone. It was not there.

Well, actually it was there, but completely hidden behind a blanket of thick fog. We knew what had happened. But that didn't lessen the impact.

Thinking back on that incident, I'm still convinced that God temporarily moved a mountain because a handful of teenage girls had a smidgen of faith in him.

Today, I find myself facing a staggering task. Dire need, like a distraught father, begs me to do something. Sharp reality, like a mountain, taunts me with my utter inability to accomplish the impossible.

I look around for help, experts who can guide me, volunteers who can come alongside me. "Maybe we can pool our efforts," I think. But then I realize that, like Jesus' followers of long ago, I live among (and stand in the front of the line of) an *"unbelieving and perverse generation" (Matt. 17:17 NIV)*. We aren't seeing impossibly good things happen in people's lives because we who serve the true God have only microscopic faith.

In my mind's eye, I stand again on the path where I stood so many years ago. I gaze at the mountain that seems so immovable and pray to the God who can do any miracle effortlessly, "Increase my faith!"

Snapshot 70

□

Hot Pursuit

These days, *passion* is a hot topic. Whether we're talking business, hobbies, love life, or church work, someone's sure to raise the cry, "Pursue your passion!"

Good advice, I'd say. Too many people pursue nothing. They just do what's expected, then vegetate for awhile in front of the TV before going to bed, getting up, and doing what's expected again.

Too many others run from the things they should run toward, refusing to take the risk of grasping for what they believe to be out of reach.

We're inspired by stories of passionate souls who accomplished the impossible because of an unconquerable inner drive. We applaud the athletes, the entrepreneurs, the vocalists whose passion for what they do has taken them to the top. We salute the "average person" whose passionate stand for a cause rallies others and effects change. We follow the rare leaders whose words convey a passion we can almost taste.

So, hey, I'd say, pursue your passion. But I might be telling you wrong. In fact, Proverbs 14:30 says rather frankly, *"Passion is rottenness to the bones" (NASU).*

Being a woman heading upward from middle age, I do not want rottenness in my bones. Nor do I want a ho-hum life, characterized by ennui. (Ever since high school, when I studied *Thirty Days to a More Powerful Vocabulary,* I've been looking for a place to use that word.) So, hey, if I don't pursue my passion, won't my life prove boring and unsatisfying?

It would seem so. But consider the wise king Solomon, a man of passion if ever there was one. Among Solomon's passions were women and (of all things) buildings. Like the old woman in the shoe, Solomon had so many of both he didn't know what to do. Starting with one temple and one house, Solomon built *"whatever he desired to build" (1 Kings 9:19 NIV)* including whole cities. He married 1,000 first and second-class wives.

After a long life and good reign, he ended up, not satisfied, but empty; not fulfilled, but frustrated and at odds with his people and his God. His subjects spoke of him as the king who *"put a heavy yoke on us"* *(1 Kings 12:10 NIV)*. God said (Brunt paraphrase): "He lost the ballgame in the last inning." All because Solomon pursued his passions.

So what does that mean for us? Well, if the wisest king in the world ran amuck in hot pursuit, I suspect we can too. Even if the things we seek are good, unbridled pursuit of passion will inevitably leave us groveling before gods that exist only in our minds.

So what should we do? Okay, here's my revised advice, first found in 1 Timothy 6:11: *"Pursue righteousness, godliness, faith, love, endurance and gentleness" (NIV)*.

"What?" you say. "Won't that mean, like, utter dullsville?" If you have to ask, you obviously haven't tried it.

The pursuit of godliness is the risk of all risks. It's an agonizing, utterly impossible pursuit, yet it does not lead to frustration. It leads to completeness. Somewhere along the way, this pursuit will almost surely demand we go the opposite direction from our passion.

At the crossroad moment, you'll probably have zero incentive for choosing righteousness over passion. In fact, you may be laughing at me for even suggesting that you do so. I've stood at that crossroad, and I'm still waving sad farewells to deep desires.

Even so, I've decided to live in hot pursuit of the righteousness that comes from knowing the only true God. Will you join me? Along the way, we just may encounter a new—and purer—passion.

◻

The Heartbreak of Hair Rebellion

"So how's the move going?" people ask.

"Well, I'm doing fine," I'm tempted to tell them, "but I don't know if my hair's going to make it."

Men won't understand this. But women know that relocation almost always provokes hair rebellion. It often shows up the first time you try a new hairdresser. This hairdresser may come highly recommended by every woman in North America, but—count on it—he or she will not be able to tame your hair. You will leave the hairdressing establishment with plans to hide in your closet for the next three months.

When we moved to Indiana, it took me two years to find a beautician to whom my hair would succumb. Then, she disappeared.

I called one day to make an appointment, only to hear, "Linda isn't here anymore." Afterward, I tried valiantly to track Linda down but couldn't locate her anywhere. I suspect that my hair, angry at being conquered, had sent her anonymous threats, scaring her so badly she fled the country.

Regardless how it happened, I was bereft of beautician. When, at last, I found a second person capable of taking my hair in hand, we moved again. Now in Oklahoma, I'm putting off my First Hair Appointment as long as possible, but to no avail. My locks have already begun rebelling in other ways.

In case you don't know, Oklahoma is windy. In particular, the parking lot of my office building is windy. No matter what pains I may take each morning to create a stylish do, the moment I step from my car, the wind taunts and, like a child unable to resist a playmate's call, my hair cavorts, throwing itself into instant disarray that refuses to be corrected.

Truth is, even without the wind, my hair takes great pride in pretending it's going to look okay, only to wilt or kink as soon as I put down the brush. Yet all this I could take—if only my unruly hair were not falling out.

It's true. As much as I want to live in denial, my brush and my bathroom floor force me to admit: my tresses are engaged in the ultimate rebellion. They're self-destructing while I stand helplessly by.

This isn't the first time this has happened. Shortly after we moved to Indiana, I got a perm. Afterward (while hiding in the closet), I occasionally brushed my hair, only to find that most of my hair remained in the brush. When I accused the beautician of over-perming me and so promoting baldness, she said, "That perm wouldn't have caused your hair to fall out. Have you been under a lot of stress lately?"

I thought I was handling the stress associated with moving rather well. But my hair had found me out. And here it is, happening again!

Jesus asked a question about birds that somehow applies here. He said, *"Are not two sparrows sold for a cent? And yet not one of them will fall to the ground apart from your Father."* Then, he added, *"But the very hairs of your head are all numbered. So do not fear; you are more valuable than many sparrows"* (Matt. 10:29–31 NASU).

The God who runs the universe is counting the hairs of my head (which means he's subtracting a lot lately). Fortunately, he's not alarmed, and he doesn't want me to be either. He's got the move, the stress, and even the hair rebellion under control.

He values every one of us enough to take in hand even the silly problems no one else would notice.

Snapshot 72

□

Jeremiah's Cry

Once, there lived a man who cried a lot. He wasn't a wimp, nor was he a whiner. He cried a lot because he saw clearly and what he saw alarmed him. He cried a lot because he cared deeply and the ones for whom he cared stood to lose everything.

Now, this man didn't just cry, as in weeping. He cried, as in warning. He knew the people he loved were making choices that would ultimately destroy them. They were unknowingly speeding toward a bridge that was out. He knew there was another way open to them, if they would just take it. There was a way that led to life.

The people around him thought him crazy. They thought him harsh. "Hush," they said. "We're doing fine."

And indeed, it appeared they were. They lived in a nation that had enjoyed loads of blessings for lots of years. Economically speaking, things looked okay. Most folks were making a living. Some were making a killing—financially, that is. Many had good benefits and a fair amount of vacation days. Others had discovered their own ways to make ends meet.

Of course, they did have wrenching personal and family problems. But they figured, "So does everyone else." They did have a society that seemed increasingly bent on hurting itself. But they figured, "That doesn't concern me." You see, they had become adept at watching the news and blocking out its import.

They rallied around leaders who insisted, "We can lead in opposite directions at the same time." They scratched their heads when children who'd ingested truckloads of violence from infancy began regurgitating it. They laughed at anyone who mentioned the word *consequences*.

Sadly, these folks had also become adept at playing church. Oh, it did seem fewer people came out to play these days. Some had grown tired of the game and gone home. But many still gathered on the day prescribed for worship. They didn't worship, exactly. But they put on a great show.

And they decided—unanimously—that things had gone far enough the morning the crying guy, whose name was Jeremiah, decided to do his crying right outside the church door. The guy had some nerve! He had no invitation from the pastor. He didn't wait for the special music. And he said things that were way out in left field.

I mean, there he stood, pointing his finger, not at the heathen, but at the most faithful (and affluent) church members. Okay, he was pointing at the least faithful church members, too. He was even pointing at the visitors. (Everybody knows you don't make visitors feel uncomfortable, or they'll never come back.)

Jeremiah was crying at all of them. He was telling them: *"Reform your ways!"* He was saying, *"Do not trust in deceptive words" (Jer. 7:4 NIV).* And (get this), he claimed to be speaking for God.

"I gave them this command," said God (according to Jeremiah): *"Obey me, and I will be your God and you will be my people. Walk in all the ways I command you, that it may go well with you. But they did not listen or pay attention; instead, they followed the stubborn inclinations of their evil hearts" (Jer. 7:23–24 NIV).*

"Doesn't that idiot know who we are?" the church-goers asked. "We go to church, to church, to church!"

And so, they appointed a committee to keep all cry-ers off the property. They didn't change their ways. And, ultimately, they did face the consequences. Then Jeremiah, who did see clearly and who did care deeply, really cried.

Snapshot 73

□

Rewriting the Rules

As sins go, lying is surely a little one. Marital infidelity isn't even on the list. And lying about marital infidelity may even be commendable (as long as we lie to keep from hurting the loved ones we're cheating on).

We know all this because of today's polls. Tomorrow, things may be different.

We "enlightened folk" have long suspected that some rules are just too hard for us humans to obey. Among them are several commandments a fellow named Moses supposedly got from God.

Here's a sampling of these rules: *"You shall not make for yourself an idol." "You shall not commit adultery." "You shall not give false testimony" (Ex. 20:4,14,16 NIV)*. Pretty stiff stuff.

Those of us who intend on ignoring these rules argue that they're outdated, having been concocted long before polls were invented. What's more, they're negative rules, sure to damage our delicate psyches and shatter our self-esteem.

Such rules may have worked in olden days when handed down to unenlightened vagrants (we reason), but they're simply too confining and unrealistic for modern times.

So, okay, let's take a peek at what happened in the olden days when people heard these rules. We can only hit the high spots. For the full account, check out the biblical book of Exodus, beginning with chapter 19.

For starters, God showed up on top of a mountain and spoke to millions gathered at its foot. In a display of power that scared the daylights out of everybody there, God told the people his rules. Then, he called their leader, Moses, to come up the mountain to get a written copy.

After a 40-day summit, God told Moses (Brunt paraphrase), "You'd better go back down. Your people have taken a poll." Sure enough, Moses went down to find that the people, by common consent, had already tossed out rules they'd heard God himself speak.

Apparently, they figured such commands were just too hard to obey. In Moses' absence, they found a leader willing to make ethical choices based on popular opinion. Heady with the power to rewrite the rules, Moses' own brother created a hollow, metal cow-god. Everyone celebrated by throwing a party.

Before long, the people were happily committing adultery, and their new leader was freely giving false testimony. The polls had won out, right?

Well, now, here's the odd thing: When Moses saw all this, he didn't concede defeat. He didn't apologize for promoting standards way too high for anyone to live up to. He didn't pat the offenders' heads and say, "After all, they're only human."

With vigor, Moses upheld God's standards. What's more, God upheld God's standards. He didn't change the rules. He didn't soften the requirements because everybody in the class had flunked the first test.

He wasn't being hard-nosed. He was being *holy*. He was refusing to put eternal standards up for a vote.

Today, we live in a "create your own cow-god" society. Changing moral standards like underwear, we excuse the inexcusable and suppose we can get by with it. We condone the forbidden and assume we won't be called to account. Meanwhile, we conduct polls just to make sure we all agree our new rules are okay.

We have plenty of leaders willing to build sacred cows for us. They govern by approval rating. And the few leaders who show integrity? Those, we decry. They cramp our style—and this makes us furious.

But when we hurtle past God's rules, intent on doing our own thing, we accomplish roughly the same thing as a crowd who, by consensus, run off a cliff, believing gravity will not effect them.

Snapshot 74

□

Cruel Joke

Dear Mr. Magazine Customer Service Person:

I'm sure you don't remember our phone conversation. For one thing, you talk to hundreds of people a day. For another thing, what I asked you to do hasn't happened.

I know you understood my request. What you didn't understand was why. "You want to cancel your subscription because of one joke?" you asked, incredulous.

"Yes, and since the subscription was a gift from my mother, please refund the difference to her."

Immediately after talking with you, I called my mom to explain what I'd done. When her refund arrived, I didn't want her to think me an ungrateful wretch. Thing is, she hasn't received her refund. And I continue to receive a new issue of your publication each month.

So I'm writing to tell you I meant it—and to try again to explain why.

First, let me say I appreciate the fact that you think highly of the publication that pays your salary. Millions of other people think highly of it also.

But let's just suppose that you were on the scene in one of the World Trade Center towers on September 11, 2001. When a jet slammed into the tower, you were knocked unconscious by falling debris. Everyone else was rushing out past you, but one man stopped to see if you were breathing. Discovering that you were, he hoisted you onto his back and carried you down who-knows-how-many flights of stairs to safety. Re-entering the building, he helped several others to safety. When the tower collapsed, he was inside.

Now let's suppose that, some months later, your fine publication which so many people read and admire, printed a joke in its well-known joke column making fun of the way this man died. How do you suppose you would feel? What do you think you would do?

Quite a while before 9–11, someone died rescuing me. His death was the butt of your magazine's joke. Oh his name wasn't mentioned. But his identity was quite clear.

The joke referred to him as "that guy nailed to the plus sign." I know him as Jesus Christ my Lord. Men driven by hatred engineered his death; men skilled in torture carried it out.

But, just for the record, Jesus wasn't powerless before them. No, "that guy" acquiesced to the suffering and the dying for one reason: It was the only way to save you and me. He knew up front that not everyone would understand. Even before his birth, a man named Isaiah foretold his heroism this way: "Like one from whom men hide their faces he was despised, and we esteemed him not. . . . But he was pierced for our transgressions, he was crushed for our iniquities" (Isa. 53:3,5 NIV).

He died in my place, Mr. Customer Service Person. And he died in yours. He died to offer a way of escape for the man who submitted that joke and the editor who chose to publish it.

The good news is: When he went to the grave, death met its match. Though the dying was horrendous, the death was swallowed up. It held him only till the third day, and then (honest to God) he emerged—alive.

I can live without your magazine, but I cannot live—really live— without him. Nor, may I say, can you. And I will not shrug off the deep grief I feel in knowing that your publication has encouraged millions to trivialize the most incredibly selfless sacrifice anyone has ever made.

So would you please cancel my subscription. And if you have to write a reason, just put "9–11."

Sincerely,

A grieved customer

Snapshot 75

□

Elvis and Friends

My cat hangs around with Elvis Presley. Regretfully, she knew who he was long before I did.

You have to understand: Our gray, long-haired, maddeningly superior Tessa continually frustrates us in the area of relationship-building. She wants the food we give her and the occasional comfort of a leg to rub. She'll hang fairly close to a family member who's working or playing in the yard. Otherwise, she has no use for humans. She never wants to be held, rarely wants to be rubbed—and then only on her belly and only briefly.

When it comes to other animals, however, she's a turn-cat. Dropping her inhibitions, she invites everyone (including the silky black cat, the large gray cat, the scrawny gray cat, the ugly yellow cat and the black-and-white skunk) into her little cat-door in the garage to stay awhile and enjoy a bite of supper.

Those times when we make out-of-town trips and leave Tessa's food in a self-feeder, we can guess by the amount consumed that she's thrown parties for the whole neighborhood in our absence.

Tessa moved with us from Indiana to Oklahoma City three years ago. A year old at the time, she took up residence in our fenced back yard, not realizing for six months that she could climb the fence. Since then, she's gotten to know the neighborhood quite well. Maybe that's why her fellow felines feel free to drop in so often.

As of March, we didn't know our human neighbors nearly as well as Tessa knew their pets. Of the 10 households nearest us, we really knew only one couple. We had talked briefly with members of four other families. That left five families we'd never even seen.

The high school student next door mowed our yard one summer. But for all we knew, he lived by himself.

I attribute this isolation to privacy fences (which are a fact of life here), automatic garage doors, our daughters' ages and the wrenching new lifestyle we entered upon moving here. In Indiana, where we lived for four years, we had no fence, our girls were elementary age and I worked out of a home office. We soon knew everyone on the street.

Here, I work full-time outside the home. My husband has a rigorous travel schedule. And our daughters attend a Christian secondary school on the far side of town.

When we moved in, only one family came to greet us. I didn't know for a year that the next-door neighbors, whose son later mowed our yard, had moved into their house a month after we moved into ours. Doubtless, they were wondering why we hadn't come over to greet them.

So, 32 months after coming to the neighborhood, we set out to be part of it. Bearing gifts (a liter of Coke and bag of popcorn), we approached each house, rang the bell, introduced ourselves, chatted briefly and told our neighbors we were praying for them (which we are).

Everyone received us warmly. Kathy, our next-door neighbor, practically yanked us into her home. "I'm *so* glad to meet you," she cried, introducing her husband and the son we already knew. In the midst of a lovely visit, she announced, "These are our cats. That black one is Elvis Presley."

We recognized Elvis immediately. We'd shooed him out of our garage numerous times.

In the Old Testament, God said, *"Love your neighbor as yourself" (Lev. 19:18 NASU)*. It's a rule so important for our well-being that he said it again in the New Testament.

Now, I'm determined: My finicky cat will not do a better job of building neighborly relationships than I.

Snapshot 76

□

Building Monuments

Oklahoma does things to people. It made E.W. Marland a millionaire—and a pauper. The man made his fortune in oil. He built a lavish Italian Renaissance mansion in Ponca City in the 1920's, complete with ornately painted ceilings, and lived there only three years. Between the day he moved in and the day he moved out, he lost his fortune.

For the next 30 years, Marland's life had its ups and downs. He served one term as governor of Oklahoma. He lost three races for U.S. Congress. At his death, he lived in a little cottage on property adjoining the mansion. From his bed in the cottage, he continually stared through a picture window at the palace he had sold for almost nothing.

Oklahoma does things to people. It both welcomed and rebuffed homesteaders who poured into Oklahoma territory between 1889 and 1906, when treaties with Native Americans opened the land to settlement. These pioneers-come-lately (the last in the 48 contiguous states) often arrived in covered wagons and lived in sod houses, crude structures ruled by dust and insects. These homesteaders fought to tame land that alternately awed them with its beauty and destroyed them with storms and drought.

I drove most of the length of northern Oklahoma this week—one day, gawking at the ceilings in the Marland Mansion; another day, riding through miles of empty plains. At the mansion, I stood before white life-size statues of E.W. Marland's adopted son George and adopted daughter (later turned wife) Lydie.

In the plains, I pondered each place where a single stand of trees punctuated a sprawling field. Someone had told me such trees mark the spots where homesteaders tried to make it. Today, some of the trees shade modest homes. In many places, the trees stand alone.

The lonely trees, the empty mansion, the statues of a man and woman caught at the peak of youth rise as monuments to human effort—so powerful, so feeble, so ageless, so bound by time, so determined, so broken. Wafting from these monuments come the acrid smell of irony, the poignant melody of tears.

Of course, you don't have to go to Oklahoma to see such monuments. Truth is, every place does things to people. Every region in this world has its own set of wonders and beauties and harsh realities that alternately attract and repel, embrace and evict those who dwell there.

Marland lost his millions in the Great Depression—as did countless others all across the nation. Wherever pioneers have dared to go, some have made it; others have not. Any place can enrich the least prepared and impoverish the most persevering. No place is safe from life's reversals—except one.

A man named Moses described this place. He himself had a riches-to-rags story. He knew the realities both of the cushy life and the pioneer struggle. He tasted the irony and sadness that result when we pin our hopes on human effort.

But though he occasionally created memorials, Moses never tried to live in them. And he refused to spend his days gazing through picture windows at what might have been. Toward the end of his life, Moses wrote, *"The eternal God is a dwelling place, and underneath are the everlasting arms" (Deut. 33:27 NASU).*

We too can make our home in only one place where perseverance is always rewarded and hopes will never be dashed. Regardless where we live, we can climb into the arms of the God we cannot see.

Tragically, many reject that dwelling place. They're too busy building monuments.

Snapshot 77

☐

Are We Here?

Today, two women are on my mind. Within the same week, both of them uttered the same cry. Oh, they spoke from different circumstances, and they said it with different words. But their heart longings were identical and so poignant they left me almost breathless. All the more so because in their voices I heard the heart-cry of many other people, including me.

One of the women is young; the other, older. Both have tried to follow God. Yet neither is anywhere close to the place she planned to be at this point in her life. What's worse, the path ahead seems to lead farther and farther from where she longs to go.

Hearing their stories and seeing the place where today finds us all, I remember a question our two daughters used to ask when they were preschoolers. At the time, I thought the question funny. As we'd pull into the driveway on returning home from an outing, one of them would call from her rear car-seat, "Are we here?"

"Yes, we're here," I'd answer, knowing she meant, "Have we arrived? Are we home?" But then I couldn't resist saying, "You know, girls, wherever we are is *here*."

In September 2001, my daughters' question popped into my mind for the first time in years. Watching TV coverage of the terrorist attacks on New York City and Washington, D.C., I found myself asking, "Are we here?" I wasn't wondering if we'd arrived. And I wasn't laughing.

Now the question emerges again. But whether I'm looking at the place where two women are in contrast to where they thought they'd be or at a world situation that still doesn't seem real, I have to admit, "Yes, we're here."

So if *here* is not where we want to be, not where we thought we would be, if *here* is frustrating, frightening, unspeakably painful, or discouragingly mundane, how do we respond? What do we do?

Both the women on my mind have felt hopelessness, anger, grief.

167

Watching their life-plans abort, they, like Jacob, have wrestled with God. Yet they haven't turned from him. Through deep, wrenching sobs, one uttered the cry that expressed the heart of both: "I so want to be a woman of grace in all this!"

Ah, that's the longing, that's the cry that can change the course, not only of our own lives, but of history. You see, grace is all about God. It's what he alone pours out, and it's what returns to him as resounding applause, after accomplishing astounding things in the lives of those who receive it.

Isaiah 30:18–19 declares, *"God's not finished. He's waiting around to be gracious to you . . . Cry for help and you'll find it's grace and more grace. The moment he hears, he'll answer" (MSG).*

Do you find yourself at a place you didn't plan to be? Do you long to go beyond where you are? Do you ever wonder, "Am I here? How can I possibly be here?"

If so, you can let anger, frustration, grief—even monotony—sweep you under. But I'm asking you—no, I'm begging you, to stand and cry—not with brazen look and upraised fist, but with open heart and outstretched palm. It's that cry that releases into action the One the Bible calls *"the God of all grace"* *(1 Peter 5:10 NASU).*

Snapshot 78

□

The Birds

The two birds didn't know each other—which is probably best.

The more unfortunate of the two, the turkey, met his demise at the hands—paws? teeth?—of two dogs. The dogs dragged the lifeless turkey onto their front porch, leaving a fowl gift for their master.

When it was time to leave for work that morning, Barry put on his leather loafers and opened the front door. Finding a dead turkey in his path, he did what any self-respecting guy would have done: he kicked the turkey.

To his surprise, it hurt. In particular, it hurt his foot. Limping back inside, Barry found that a piece of turkey bone had pierced his loafer and lodged in his foot. He removed the bone and headed out to work.

All day, his foot hurt. The next day, Barry went to a doctor who started him on an antibiotic. By that night, however, Barry's foot had swollen twice its size and the pain had escalated. Rushed to the hospital, Barry learned that a tiny sliver of the turkey bone had lodged in his foot, creating massive infection. He was admitted to the hospital, where he received strong doses of antibiotic by IV—and turkey balloons from all his friends.

That same week, my friend Donna saw a white dove sitting on a low branch of a tree in my yard. How Donna knew the dove couldn't fly, I don't know. But she rightly assessed the fact that the cats in our neighborhood like to bring home fowl gifts just as much as Barry's dogs. What's more, cats can climb trees.

Donna reached for the dove—and found it would perch contentedly on her hand. Having far more compassion than I, she gently placed the dove in a cardboard box and took him home. Afterward, she bought an inexpensive cage and named her dove "Hootie"—"because he coos all the time."

At 4:00 one morning, Hootie was living up to his name. Unable to sleep, Donna went to Hootie's cage, opened the door and reached for the dove. "He gets quiet when you hold him," Donna says. But when Donna reached, Hootie lunged. Donna ended up holding a handful of white tail feathers. Hootie ended up with a bare rump.

Like any self-respecting gal, Donna panicked, certain she had mortally wounded her plucked bird. But, happily, Hootie lived—though the indignity and pain cooled his cooing for awhile.

All of which goes to show: Adversity appears in the strangest of places. It comes in the strangest of ways. Odds are, your mama never told you, "Don't kick a dead turkey." That's because she wasn't expecting you to encounter danger from that quarter. Nor did she caution, "Don't comfort a cooing dove." Even mamas can't always predict when solving one problem will only create a bigger one.

Should we, then, live in fear of the birds or whatever other unexpected calamity awaits? We often do. But may I suggest another option, found in Psalm 91: *"I will say of the Lord, 'He is my refuge and my fortress, my God, in whom I trust.'"*

What does profound trust in God have to do with dead turkeys and plucked doves? *"Surely he will save you from the fowler's snare and from the deadly pestilence. He will cover you with his feathers, and under his wings you will find refuge; his faithfulness will be your shield and rampart"* (vv. 2–4 NIV).

In a world of unexpected difficulties, kicking turkeys may send you to the hospital, but crawling under God's wings will give you better shelter than a mother's love.

Snapshot 79

□

Tumult

So many emotions in such a short time.

Ah, yes, you name it, within a two-week period I experienced it: loss, hope, disappointment, anticipation, dread, rejection, comfort, laughter, camaraderie, rest, exhaustion, tension, discouragement, encouragement, anger, guilt, delight, love.

Wish I could tell you the stories. But they involve people who might not appreciate the public exposure. Let me invite you to fill in your own stories—while I expose myself.

Looking back, the rejection hurt the worst. At least, it provoked the most tears. On the other side of the tears, the wound remains and, with it, an ache for people close to me who've been experiencing similar rejection for some time. Now that I've tasted what they've drunk deeply, I can empathize with them in a new way. I pray for them more fervently.

The guilt did the most destruction, yet it produced no tears. At first, I had too much fun rationalizing what I'd thought, said, and done. People had provoked my reactions. *They* were guilty, not me. Rehearsing the details of their deeds, I pronounced myself off the hook.

Inside, I felt a gnawing sense of wrongdoing. Although I buried this guilt in a back closet of my mind, I couldn't make it go away.

Finally, the clamor in the closet grew too violent to ignore. Throwing open the closet door, I discovered that the guilt I'd tried to stuff had eaten holes in my heart. I brought the things I'd tried to hide out of the closet, not in order to flaunt them, but to get rid of them. "I was wrong," I said to God and to those I'd offended.

The encouragement came in unexpected ways at unexpected times: a note handed to me with a prayer inside, a warm thank-you spoken in a hallway, a hug, a Bible verse that had always been there but today provided exactly the words needed.

Isn't it interesting that, just as hurt comes through relationships, so does help? In these two tumultuous weeks, small acts of encouragement have made an enormous difference.

Oh, and the laughter—it came unexpectedly, as well. (I'll tell you this experience since the persons involved didn't mind embarrassing me.) I had asked two men with whom I work, to do a comedy presentation at a women's conference my office was sponsoring. I expected to giggle over the guys' antics. I didn't expect them to call me to the platform.

There, they painted each fingernail of my right hand a different color. They said it was a new way to show the difference God can make in a person's life. Let me hasten to say: God can change any person's life, and I'm sure he can use multi-colored nails to illustrate how he does it. But that day in the hallway, the food line, the workshop rooms, the restroom, woman after woman asked to see my hand. When I held up a gray nail, a red one, a white one, a lime green one and a gold sparkly one, God gave us all laughter.

The same day as the nail experience, I was trying to find one of those encouraging Bible verses I'd encountered. Instead, I ran across a sentence I decided to include in a thank-you note to the guys who decorated my nails. It's the first sentence of 2 Corinthians 12:11, and it says, *"I have made a fool of myself, but you drove me to it" (NIV)*.

So many emotions in such a short time. I can't tell you how glad I am that encouragement and laughter were among them.

Snapshot 80

□

Forge Ahead

Our society has a motto. We don't think about it. We just live by it—and often we're more committed to it than to life itself. Our motto? *Forge Ahead.*

My maternal grandfather demonstrated his commitment to this maxim every time he got behind the wheel. He and my grandmother lived in Monroe, Louisiana, which in the days before interstates was an eight-hour trip from my hometown of Corinth, Mississippi. Once—and only once—I made the drive with Granddaddy. We reached our destination alive, solely by the grace of God.

In that era, we traveled two-lane highways with a maximum speed limit of 65. Part of the route wound through hill country, with many long "No Passing" stretches. Further, the route included numerous small towns with speed limits that basically required us to get out and crawl.

However, Granddaddy had a simple plan for making a road trip: Accelerate to 75 mph and never slow down for any reason. During that particular trip, we spent seven hours passing on hills, flying through stop signs, and narrowly missing so many oncoming vehicles I had to lie down in the back seat to keep from dying of a heart attack at the ripe age of 10.

Today, most of us live in the same manner that Granddaddy drove. We get up in the morning, set our cruise control on 75 mph, and barrel through the day with one agenda: Never slow down for any reason.

We hurry our kids, run over people in grocery store aisles, and honk and swear in traffic, urged onward by our all-consuming drive to get where we're going. People have left their babies in car-seats in hot cars—and not remembered their own children until too late—because the day's demands pressed them to forge ahead.

If circumstances require us to slow down—for example, if a train blocks our path—we do everything we can to find a way around it and, that failing, we curse or complain or hit something.

I was summoned to jury duty recently. May I tell you the one topic of conversation that dominated all others? As we sat in the courtroom waiting for orientation, then sat in the jury assembly room waiting to be called up, and then—when not chosen—sat some more, we, the prospective jurors of federal court in the Western District of Oklahoma, lamented loud and long the court's requirement that we be still and wait. Inwardly, we sat with motor running and foot revving the accelerator, irate that our civic duty kept us from forging ahead.

One morning not long after jury duty, I faced a frustrating situation where there seemed no right way to go. Distressed, I told a friend, "I don't know what to do." She replied, "When you don't know what to do, stop."

How impossible! How heretical! I had before me, in alphabetical order, an impressive list of reasons why I couldn't stop. And yet, my friend's words freed me to see that, sometimes, forging ahead isn't the right thing to do. Sometimes, slowing—or even stopping—is good.

A singer named David said to God in Psalm 139, *"You chart the path ahead of me and tell me where to stop and rest" (v. 3 NLT).*

Like Granddaddy on a trip, I'll miss those rest stops as long as my plan for living is: Accelerate to 75 mph and never slow down for any reason. But if, like David, I'll keep my eyes on God, he'll show me when to keep moving and when to make no move at all.

Snapshot 81

□

Bouncers, Rollers and Plodders

It's traumatic to go through life with low energy. Tiring, too.

Some people bounce and bubble. Others are like steamrollers—always moving relentlessly forward. The bouncers and the rollers are different in lots of ways, but they have one thing in common: energy.

I suppose these types do run out of steam sometime in the middle of the night. But we plodders never notice: We've all been asleep for hours. And we're still asleep when the Energizer Bunnies jump up to go at it again.

A bouncer skips over life's hurdles. A roller plows them down. Meanwhile, we plodders find ourselves stalled and thwarted time and again.

One steamroller woman who lived a century ago kept such a phenomenal schedule that her biographer got tired just writing about her. The biographer called her *indefatigable,* which doesn't mean "incapable of getting fat," but rather "incapable of fatigue." (Though, come to think of it, tireless people do tend to burn off weight, rather than accumulate it.)

Like other steamrollers, this indefatigable lady spent her long and full life wondering why everyone else couldn't keep up with her. I, by contrast, have spent many days wondering how everyone else could keep going.

Two trips stand out in my mind: one to Baldwin, Mississippi; the other, to Moscow, Russia. In both situations, I spent a week or more working alongside a group of people who were there solely to help meet needs of other people. Both times, halfway through the week, I was exhausted. I had to take a rest break in order to finish the task.

It wasn't a case of age creeping up on me. The first time, I was in my 20s. The second time, in my mid-30s.

The awful, irrefutable truth is: I'm a plodder. I take my vitamins. I walk regularly. God has given me good health. But I have limited energy. I simply can't go far without refueling.

That's why I'm always caught off guard when people ask me, "How do you do so much?"

From my perspective, it often seems I'm not accomplishing anything. One afternoon, I sat at my desk, utterly frustrated and totally drained. I told a friend, "It feels like I've been trying to run in quicksand."

But when I reach the end of the month and look back, I'm usually amazed to see how much has gotten done. Though utterly unable to leap tall buildings, I somehow end up on the other side of them. Though anything but a superwoman, I sometimes appear to have accomplished super feats.

So the next time someone asks, "How do you do it?" I'm going to offer the answer first given a few millennia ago: *"Do you not know? Have you not heard? The Lord is the everlasting God, the Creator of the ends of the earth. He will not grow tired or weary, and his understanding no one can fathom. He gives strength to the weary and increases the power of the weak"* (Isa. 40:28–29 NASU).

It's not that I'm trying to be humble or spiritual. I'm simply acknowledging the truth: When a plodder soars—or even walks without fainting—she knows the strength she's displaying comes from somewhere besides herself. And when she's crying out to the indefatigable God for what she knows she does not have, it's obvious when he's supplying.

Yes, it's traumatic to face the relentless demands of life with low energy. But trauma turns to triumph when, shouldering the task, I find myself *"struggling with all his energy, which so powerfully works in me"* (Col. 1:29 NIV).

Snapshot 82

□

Unsolved Mysteries

It's a mystery—at least to me and the other women in my workplace. We discuss it sometimes.

"Why does that happen?" we ask.

We're referring, of course, to the faucet that controls the cold water at the right-hand sink in the third-floor ladies restroom. You turn it off. It immediately comes back on. Not a trickle, mind you; but a full-fledged flow.

This may happen once or—in my experience—up to seven times before you finally prevail and the thing stays off. I've met feisty faucets before, but this is the first totally rebellious one.

All you plumber types may have the riddle solved without even seeing the sink, but for those of us who use the faucet daily, the mystery remains.

My neighbor, Kathy, has an even greater mystery. It involves, not faucets, but cell phones. Kathy and her business partner, Laura, were driving in Laura's car, discussing a mutual friend. In the course of the conversation, they thought they heard a tiny voice calling Laura's name.

Laura checked her cell phone. Nobody there. Kathy didn't check her cell phone because she never has it with her. She keeps it in her car—turned off. (Why? Ah, that too is a mystery.)

Anyway, the two tried to continue their conversation. Still, a tiny voice kept calling, "Laura! Laura, are you there?" Finally, Kathy grabbed up her purse and opened it. To her amazement, her cell phone was inside. To her further amazement, it was turned on and a voice was emitting from it.

Ah, but here's the clincher—the real mystery. The tiny voice belonged to the mutual friend that Kathy and Laura had been discussing. This friend's phone had rung. She had answered—only to hear Laura and Kathy talking about her. While she kept trying to get their attention, she heard their whole conversation.

Kathy is happy to report that she and Laura did not say anything inappropriate about their friend. But be warned: You never know who's listening. And you never know how.

I mean, who put Kathy's cell phone in her purse, turned it on, and dialed the number of the very friend whose name was on her lips?

It's a mystery to me when water faucets and cell phones seem to have a mind of their own. It's a mystery to God when people he created rebel against him.

How can anything be a mystery to the God who knows everything? Beats me. But God discusses his consternation quite a bit in the Bible's pages. *"Why do you persist in rebellion?"* he asks *(Isa. 1:5 NIV)*. *"Why do my people say, 'We are free to roam; we will come to you no more'?" (Jer. 2:31 NIV).* *"Why then have these people turned away?" (Jer. 8:5 NIV).* *"Why do you go about so much, changing your ways?" (Jer. 2:36 NIV).* *"Why bring such great disaster on yourselves? . . . You will destroy yourselves and make yourselves an object of cursing and reproach" (Jer. 44:7,8 NIV).* *"Why will you die?" (Ezek. 33:11 NIV).*

Even when people dismiss him as not really there, God keeps calling their names and crying out words like these from Psalm 81: *"If you will only listen! Only test me! Open your mouth wide and see if I won't fill it. You will receive every blessing you can use!" (vv. 8,10 TLB).*

It's funny (to a point) when a faucet rebels or a cell phone makes its own calls. It's tragic when people reject the one who offers them the difference between life and death, blessing and cursing. It's more than waste, more than embarrassment. It's a mystery even God hasn't solved.

Snapshot 83

□

Crushed

I planned to turn the man off.

He started talking in mid-sentence when I started the car, his message erupting from the radio station that had featured music when last I'd listened. His voice didn't capture me. It was flat and a little nasal, and I wasn't in the mood for someone to talk at me.

Still, the job of getting out of the parking lot and safely into oncoming traffic occupied both my hands for several moments. By then, the man with the nasal voice had begun telling about a science experiment he'd seen as a child.

It seems his teacher had heated an open, empty metal gasoline can over a bunsen burner until it was very hot. Then, the teacher had quickly capped the can, set it aside and continued with the lesson for the day. The man vividly recalled what happened next.

As the can cooled, it began to snap and contort. Suddenly, it bent inward, like someone doubled over with a blow to the stomach. Crushed—apparently by nothing—it toppled to the floor.

The science teacher used the experiment to teach about air pressure. As a faithful science teacher probably taught each of us, hot air takes up more space than cold air. Thus, as the hot air inside the can cooled, it contracted.

With nothing occupying much of the space in the can, the normal atmospheric pressure outside the can was able to crush it. If the container had been opened so that more air could rush in to replace the shrinking air inside, the can would have remained intact.

The man telling the story had his own application. He said, "In the lives of people today, it's the vacuum, not the pressure, that crushes."

Yes, we live in a high-pressure society. The speed of life presses on us. The difficulties of life press on us. The inequities of life press on us. But every generation that has lived has experienced great pressure. Just as air pressure is normal, life pressures are normal.

Yet pressure—even intense pressure—doesn't have to crush us. It's when we become empty inwardly that we can no longer cope with the things pressing on us outwardly. And, for the most part, our society is empty. We lie like a man with the breath knocked out of him, pummeled mercilessly by the repeated blows of daily living. Where past generations were resilient, we're battered.

Thousands of years ago, another battered generation heard a God-spokesman named Jeremiah cry, *"Thus says the Lord, 'What injustice did your fathers find in Me, that they went far from Me and walked after emptiness and became empty?'" (Jer. 2:5 NASU).*

Stubbornly, tragically, that generation refused to uncap the lid. Remaining empty, they were soon crushed.

Later, another God-spokesman named Paul urged, *"Be filled with the Spirit" (Eph. 5:18 NASU).* The phrase "be filled" is not a once-and-you're-done verb. It's a time-and-again verb. Like breathing, inner filling must happen continually. In fact, Paul spent his life helping people learn how to inhale the breath of God deeply and repeatedly.

This God still offers, not an escape from the pressures of life, but the inner strength to withstand them. Problem is, he's issuing his invitation to a closed-cap generation. While he's ready to fill the void, most aren't ready to open up to him.

I reached my destination before the man with the nasal voice finished speaking. And I sat in my car, crying for those all around me who will topple, crushed, rather than admit their emptiness and be filled.

Snapshot 84

□

Taking Snapshots

Want to see my pictures from last week? Look closely now. I'll have a question for you afterward.

That's the first jury room. Larger than you expected? Several hundred of us were packed into all those rows of benches. Perry Mason would have dismissed some of us for dress-code reasons. However, the guys wearing ball caps did remove them when the judge entered.

No, the judge didn't sit behind that official-looking judge's "bench." He stood there briefly to admonish us: "What you're doing is critical to our form of government. It's what sets us apart from every other nation."

See me on the far left with the soft-sided briefcase? Properly admonished, I spent the day working on the papers in that briefcase. No, I wasn't taking my duties lightly, just waiting for my name to be called.

Ready for the next picture? I pass those mimosa trees every morning on my way to meet whatever the day holds. Last week, I couldn't stop admiring them. Blooming mimosas, with their frondy leaves and wispy pink blossoms, never cease to delight me.

Okay, there's the second jury room. Small, huh? And, boy, was it crowded. They didn't have enough folding chairs to hold the hundred or so of us sent to juvenile court on Tuesday. Yes, that's me sitting on that small table next to two other ladies.

That day? Oh, I waited again—chatted with the two ladies, read a book, visited the snack room. Ah, see the lady with the big wooden box. She drew my name, told me to go home for the rest of the day and come back on Thursday.

That's me entering the juvenile building on Thursday. Do I look a bit tense? I'd really hoped to leave town early Friday afternoon for a retreat. Now, the prospects of retreating are looking rather dim.

That's me coming out of the juvenile building on Thursday. Do I look a bit more relaxed? They left us sitting in that little jury room again for a long time before a lady arrived to announce that the case had been settled and we were all dismissed.

More mimosas—a whole forest of them. We passed them on the way to the retreat.

Here are several shots of the retreat center, nestled in the Jack Fork Mountains. That's the pull-out couch where I slept. See how the corners of the egg-crate mattress are turning up under the sheet. I asked my friends, "If the whole thing rolls up with me in it, will I be an egg-roll?"

There's the cozy room where we met. Oh, and my favorite spot: the rocking chair on the wrap-around porch where I sat looking out on the evergreen forest—until the mad mud-dauber attack.

Okay, one more shot of blooming mimosas near my friend's farm. We made a pit stop there on the way home from the retreat.

So now, I have one quick question: Did you see him? He's in every picture. The odd thing is: Some people see him clearly. Some can't spot him at all. Look again. Carefully.

In Matthew 28:20, Jesus told his followers (of which I'm one), *"Be sure of this—that I am with you always, even to the end of the world" (TLB).*

Sometimes at the moment, I miss him, too. But looking back, I see that, yes, he was there. And not just standing idly by, but actively involved in random jury selection, blooming mimosas, mountaintop retreats.

Next week, I'll have a whole new batch of pictures. Don't have a clue what they'll hold—except him.

Snapshot 85

□

Prudent Stop

Yes, sir. I heard you toot your horn. I see you in my rearview mirror, throwing up your hands, wearing a frown below your brown mustache. I know you wanted me to gun it through the yellow light that would have turned red while I was in the intersection.

You would have run the light right behind me. No big deal when the alternative is waiting the long two or three minutes until it turns green again.

Please don't get me wrong. I've pulled my share of stunts on the streets and interstates of Oklahoma City since moving here. The police could have seriously improved the city's financial situation simply by following me around.

The unspoken competition, the challenge to outrun and out-maneuver all the other drivers, overtakes me more times than I'd like to admit. I'm competitive by nature. And I'm out of my element. I've spent most of my life driving two-lane backroads. A year into this rush-hour madness, I'm still tense, unsure, seduced by the strong pull to prove myself to these city folk with the witty license plates.

So, hey, while you sit back there fuming at me, I'm not judging you. But I'm not sorry I stopped. You see, sir, I'm determined to make some improvement in this area, although you obviously don't see it as improvement. I'm determined to quit trying to measure up to the standard of speed or bravado you might impose on me (or I might impose on myself) and to strive for the standard of prudence.

Yes, I realize I've just used a discarded word. *Prudence* sounds too much like *prudish* to be in vogue these days. Nobody even says it, much less desires it. And, until I consulted my *American Heritage Dictionary,* I would have been hard-pressed to tell you what it means.

Now I know that a prudent person is "wise in handling practical matters; exercising good judgment or common sense." My dictionary also says prudence "implies not only caution but also the capacity for judging in advance the probable results of one's actions."

In the book of Proverbs, a man a whole lot wiser than either of us said twice (as if to underscore its importance): *"The prudent see danger and take refuge, but the simple keep going and suffer for it" (27:12 NIV, also see 22:3).*

Sitting here at this red light, I see a dangerous result of running it, besides the dangers of getting hit or getting a ticket. You've noticed this young lady sitting beside me? She's my 14-year-old daughter. In 19 months, she'll turn 16. She's counting the days until she'll have driver's license in hand. Meanwhile, whether she admits it or not, she's watching me. If I do something questionable, she's going to make a mental note that it's all right.

She'll have plenty of opportunities to do really dumb things during the rest of her teenage years (whether behind the wheel or not). My continual heart-cry is that I won't influence her toward any of those dumb things. My constant prayer is, "Please, God, don't let me lead her toward disaster."

She heard your honk. She's seen me make wrong moves in traffic. She's heard me ask forgiveness for them. But today, you unknowingly underscored the fact that I did something right. While you tapped your steering wheel, she grabbed my hand. While you scowled, she smiled.

So, yes sir, your honk taught me a lesson, sir. It reminded me that prudence may not be fashionable, but it's still wise.

Snapshot 86

◻

Don't Toss Your Teens

Did you know we have teenage daughters? Two of them. They were not always teens—and will not always be. However, they've been daughters since birth.

This doesn't seem quite fair to my husband, who must daily learn how to live life as the only male in our household. Yes, he did grow up with two sisters, which may have prepared him somewhat. But in those days, he and his dad could commiserate.

So now, did I say we have teenage daughters? Folks warned us this time would come.

When the girls were newborn and going off like little alarm clocks all through the night, people said, "Just wait till they're teenagers." When the two were toddlers, finding their way into all the places we didn't want them to go, people said, "Just wait till they're teenagers." When they refused to wear the clothes I'd bought for them, came down with every childhood illness right on cue, mourned for every cat we had that perished, got in spats with friends, got in spats with each other, and did what we specifically told them not to do—people said, "Just wait till they're teenagers."

We couldn't wait. We thought these kind folks were telling us that, on the magic day our girls turned 13, all their problems (and ours) would disappear.

As you've probably figured out, it didn't happen that way.

But you know what else didn't happen? I didn't suddenly dislike our daughters.

In fact, I like them a lot. So does my husband (even if they are girls). And I can still say this even after the last two weeks, which have been, let us say, tumultuous.

Teenage girls (and guys, too, I'm told) live on a roller coaster. Rather like riding Space Mountain at Disney World, they zoom ahead in the dark, never knowing when they're going to ratchet uphill, fall off a cliff, turn

185

180 degrees, or actually roll along level track for a time. Warning to parents: Whatever path your daughter's roller coaster takes, you'll usually find yourself riding along.

This can get especially hairy if you have more than one teen in residence because, alas, each is riding a different roller coaster. When one's at the top of the hill, the other may be plummeting. When one's just leveled out, the other's rounding a breakneck curve. All of which can contribute to a diagnosis of schizophrenia in Parents of Teens (also known as POT, as in the comment, "Have you seen Deborah lately? Poor dear. She's going to POT.")

Yesterday evening, I took a walk with one daughter. With the sun hanging low in the west, we rounded the tiny lake near our home and talked about things that were on her mind. Later, riding in the car with the other daughter, I laughed with her in the deepening darkness over experiences she'd had at school that day.

Still later, snuggling on the bed in the master bedroom, the three of us read a short passage from the Bible, talked briefly, and prayed together. Our talk included serious comments about what we'd just read, thoughts from the day at large, and silly teasing (which I, of course, did not participate in because I am *never* silly).

The Message version of Psalm 127:3 says, *"Don't you see that children are God's best gift?"* It doesn't say, " . . . until they reach puberty."

When you board a roller coaster, what do you do with your valuables? Only a fool would throw them to the wind. Right here in the big middle of our girls' teenage years, I'm spending a lot of time hugging the exquisite gifts God has given.

Snapshot 87

□

Deborah P. Bread

Something deep within me cries to be unflappable. But something deeper always flaps.

My assignment was not a difficult one: meet a friend for lunch. She suggested a deli which I vaguely recalled passing but where I'd never before eaten.

Armed with a few simple directions and a cell phone number in case I got lost, I found the place easily enough. My friend walked over as I stepped from my car. The rest should have been easy: order lunch, pay for it, get it, eat it.

Ah, but the menu took up most of one wall. Facing a young lady who stood, pen and pad in hand, I heard a cacophony of soups, salads, sandwiches, and specials shrieking, "Pick me! Pick me!" "What would you like?" she asked.

Unable to answer yet, I asked her questions of my own. Pen still poised, she answered my queries; her words, polite; her tone, a tad impatient. Before my mind had fully decided, it heard my voice placing an order. The young lady wrote on the pad, tore off a page, handed it to me, and then turned to my friend, who had a whole new set of questions waiting.

Standing with paper in hand, not knowing what to do next, I felt a flap coming. The young lady hadn't asked me for money. There was no cash register at the door. "Maybe I'm supposed to pay when my order's ready," I thought.

On the far side of the long room stood a drink machine flanked by cups. I crossed the room, poured myself ice water and then turned back to find my friend. She stood at a counter mid-way between where we had ordered and the drink machine. Walking toward her, I was about to ask where she wanted to sit when she asked, "Did you pay yet?"

"You're supposed to pay here," said the young man behind the counter. He spoke loudly and more than a tad impatiently, eyeing the water I'd dared to pour before forking over the cash. Now, I was definitely flapped. Setting my purse on the counter, I dug out my credit card and handed it to him.

While he ran the card through the machine, my eyes fell on a mound of tiny loaves of bread, each separately wrapped. Banana bread? I wondered. Nut bread of some sort? Then, I spotted a small sign near the loaves that read, "Tea Bread." Bread to eat with tea? Bread made from tea?

I was still pondering that sign when the young man handed me the credit card receipt and a pen. At the appropriate place for signing, I wrote, "Deborah P. Bread."

A lovely name. A respectable name. But not my name. At least, not the last time I checked.

Okay, so I'm not cool, calm and collected on all occasions. The more flustered I become, the more dumb things I'm liable to do. But here's where Ecclesiastes 3:4 rides to the rescue. It says there is *"a time to laugh" (NASU).* In those times, appreciating what's laughable is even more important than being unflappable.

Seeing my goof, I burst out laughing—or, as Psalm 126:2 puts it, my *"mouth was filled with laughter" (NASU).* When I told the guy behind the counter what I'd done, he couldn't quite bring himself to actually laugh, but even he grinned. At least he knew he was dealing, not with a thief, but with a flapper.

As I edited the name on my credit card receipt, he leaned over and whispered charitably, "We'll just keep this between you and me."

Snapshot 88

□

The Family Plan

It was a plan destined for disaster. For one thing, it required perfect weather—not too hot nor cold, not rainy or snowy and (here's a biggy) not extremely windy. It simply wouldn't have worked during a tornado or thunderstorm or any reasonable facsimile thereof.

Further, this was a family plan, thus requiring that all family members be present. With our four busy schedules, in addition to the schedules of the people with whom we were coordinating, we found one open Friday in October. If that didn't work, we'd have to postpone indefinitely.

And there was more reason to prepare for a train wreck. My husband and I told our two teenage daughters to leave the day open and to invite a friend apiece to go on a mystery trip. Before we executed the plan, one daughter knew what was up, but the other three girls were still guessing.

The plan did not include shopping, going to a movie, renting a video, or "hanging out." Well, technically it included hanging out—but with parents. It didn't involve fast-paced activities, daring stunts, or boys. In fact, this plan ran great risk of being labeled "boring."

So why did I look forward so much to carrying it out?

The day came. Early afternoon, we drove northwest out of Oklahoma City into flat prairie land. As we drove, we talked. Our older daughter told us about a game one of her school teachers had described. This teacher's family lives in the country and enjoys "cow tippin'." That is, someone sneaks up on a sleeping cow and tries to hit the cow just right so that it falls over.

We discussed other important subjects without revealing the mystery. Finally, when the girls lay faint from suspense, we came to a house with a covered wagon standing outside. We tumbled out of the car, exchanged introductions with the family who owned the wagon, clambered aboard, and took off at roughly three miles per hour down the dirt backroads of Garfield County, Oklahoma.

This covered wagon was not an exact replica of pioneer days—but close enough for us. It had several modern conveniences, including rubber tires (as opposed to wooden wheels), folding chairs (which we learned could tip over in tight turns), a rear-view mirror (for spotting ambushes, I suppose) and a port-a-potty (which no one used).

Red-haired mules named Tom and Jerry pulled the wagon. Just for the record: They did not seem stubborn. We particularly liked it when we decided to make a 180-degree turn, and they walked backward, swinging the wagon around.

While Tom and Jerry plodded along, we chatted, sang, and enjoyed the sights (including deer and wild turkey tracks and a cemetery from land-rush days, circa 1900). At one point, the girls walked behind the wagon. That came to an abrupt halt when the mules began decorating the roadway.

At ride's end, we clambered out of the covered wagon and crossed the yard to a chuck wagon, where dinner had been cooking on an open pit.

As the sun set on a gorgeous fall day, we sat outside around card tables (like the early settlers) chatting with new friends and eating smothered steak, mashed potatoes, black-eyed peas, biscuits and homemade jelly, and cherry cobbler. (The girls helped make the biscuits and cobbler.)

On the drive home, the day got rave reviews—even from the teens.

As I said, it was a plan destined for disaster. But destiny wasn't in charge. God was. Borrowing from Psalm 20:4, *"May he give you the desire of your heart and make all your plans succeed" (NIV).*

Snapshot 89

❑

The World of
Quick and Easy

A map of the interstate system in Oklahoma City looks rather like an extended tic-tac-toe board: three highways running east to west (or four, if you count the turnpike) and three running north to south.

We live at the northwest corner of this interstate system. Thus, when Amanda asked to go to a ballgame at the southeast corner, we had a lively family discussion as to the best route to take. She ended up going the way I recommended—and encountered significant delay as a result of roadwork.

For two days, I berated myself for entering the discussion and, thus, causing our daughter to go the wrong way. Then, I myself was driving across Oklahoma City via a different route—and also encountered road construction.

These two incidents, happening as they did in the same week, prompted two questions I'm still pondering: (1) Is it possible to go from one end of Oklahoma City to another without being delayed by roadwork? (2) If you go the way you believe best—and encounter delay or difficulty— does that mean the way you chose is wrong?

We live in a highly pragmatic society. To our way of thinking, a course is the right one if we can complete it quickly and easily. In games and races, the winner is the fastest; the loser, the slowest. Even on vacations, we just aren't given to the scenic route.

What's more, we view any difficulty or setback as an obvious indicator that we goofed. If a path is the right one, travel along it should go without a hitch.

But if we follow this assumption to its logical end, we're left with a life of microwave meals. Home cooking and cakes made from scratch are out. We're also left without any new inventions or medical breakthroughs, because all such things take an inordinate amount of time and much trial-and-error.

In the world of quick and easy, we can dismiss any formal education beyond kindergarten. We can eject any kind of sports or athletic training. We can release all military personnel. And we can take the United States out of any history books.

If earlier generations had believed that the right way is the quickest and easiest: The Pilgrims would have gone back to England. The patriots would not have forfeited their lives and property to fight for independence. Lewis and Clark would not have made their famous expedition. The transcontinental railroads would never have been laid. The West would never have been settled.

You see, in the world of quick and easy, there are no pioneers. There is no stamina or tenacity. There is no taking of difficult terrain.

One pioneer named Paul said in 2 Corinthians 6: "*We patiently endure troubles and hardships and calamities of every kind. We have been beaten, been put in jail, faced angry mobs, worked to exhaustion, endured sleepless nights, and gone without food*" (*vv. 4–5 NLT*).

If you and I set out in a certain direction—and ran into the difficulties Paul faced—we'd assume we were on the wrong track. After that first beating, we'd take another look at the map to find a better route.

But Paul didn't let difficulty or delay dictate the way. He said, "*Since God in his mercy has given us this wonderful ministry, we never give up*" (*2 Cor. 4:1 NLT*).

Here on the Oklahoma City tic-tac-toe board, our daughter didn't reach the ballgame at the time she desired, but with a little perseverance she got there. Now, her mama is learning not to judge a route by its roadwork.

Snapshot 90

□

The Edge of Guilt

"The wicked are edgy with guilt, ready to run off even when no one's after them," says Proverbs 28:1 (MSG).

This proverb is true. Don't ask me how I know. Okay, I'll tell you.

The weekend had been memorable—Paris in the spring. Paris, Texas, that is—where my friend Dottie and I had attended a Christian women's conference. We'd driven several hours toward home, stopping once for gas, once again an hour later to eat supper.

After the meal, we walked to the front of the restaurant to pay. I reached in my purse for my credit card and realized it wasn't in the designated slot. Vaguely, I remembered putting the card in my pocket.

My hand located the card about the time my brain recalled why it was there. "Dottie," I said.

"Did you lose your card?" she asked.

"No," I answered weakly, smiling at the cashier. Slowly but surely, it was all coming back: We'd pulled into that gas station a couple of hours earlier, and Dottie had run for the restroom. Desperately needing to do the same, I elected instead to pump the gas first.

Expecting to pay at the pump, I had credit card in hand. I slid the card into my pocket upon realizing that I had to pay inside. After pumping the gas, I was heading toward the building when Dottie emerged, looking frantic and asking, "Can we go somewhere else to the restroom?"

"Sure," I said. We got into the car and drove off.

Two hours later, I exited a restaurant, crying, "I've robbed a gas station!"

"I'm an accomplice!" Dottie wailed. Anything can happen when two women get desperate.

Do not call the police. I've already turned myself in. But not before finding out just how edgy guilt can make you.

Weary from travel, longing to get home and having no idea how to contact the station, I called my husband. Our daughter Amanda took the call. Then, she calmly told her daddy, "Mama robbed a gas station, and she's laughing."

Okay, I *was* laughing. But it wasn't happy laughing—it was edgy laughing. Jerry, on the other hand, wasn't laughing. I gave him several clues for locating the place and asked him to report the crime.

A few minutes later, I called again to see if he'd done so. "I don't think he's tried yet," said our daughter. "He's fixing hamburgers."

That's when extreme edginess erupted. While he grilled out, we were fleeing the crime scene in a car owned by the Christian organization for which I work. Probably, the gas station attendant had already traced the license number.

"My prints are on the bathroom key," Dottie said.

"And they saw your face, not mine," I added. "If we're stopped, I'll tell them you abducted me."

We almost ran off the road when a police car passed us. Later, when I dropped Dottie at her house, she asked, "Do you want me to call ahead to see if the coast is clear?" By then, I was sure that if the cops weren't waiting for me at my house, they'd be outside my workplace on Monday morning.

Arriving home, I discovered my husband had already talked with the folks at the station. They thanked him for calling and said to send a check for the gas. "Do you want our phone number?" he asked. "No," they answered.

Ah, the relief when that check was in the mail! Proverbs 28:1 ends: *"Honest people are relaxed and confident, bold as lions" (MSG)*. Thankfully, that's true too.

Snapshot 91

□

Two Icy Nights

Some moments masquerade as eternity. They happen so emphatically you think you'll be living them forever. Even when long gone, they leave an indelible mark you may not always be conscious of but never can quite get rid of.

In 2002, one of those permanent moments in my life did something rather amazing. It repeated itself. While an entirely new evening was unfolding, a hauntingly familiar one was resurfacing. Eight years melted away, leaving two parallel nights twisted inextricably together.

The first night was a Thursday—February 10, 1994, to be exact. The second night was a Wednesday—January 30, 2002. The first incident happened in Corinth, Mississippi. The second, in Oklahoma City. In both situations, sleet or freezing rain had fallen all day. Weather forecasters were declaring, "Ice Storm Warning."

Both times, my husband was out of town. My daughters and I were home. Since I was the oldest, I was in charge.

The first time, I was blissfully ignorant. While we listened to sleet tapping against the windows and, later, to the shotgun sounds of branches snapping off nearby trees, it never occurred to me to be concerned about the power.

The second time, I drove to a local convenience store to get firewood—just didn't get enough.

Both times, our power went out about dusk. Both times, we had only the fireplace to rely on for heat. Both times, we had one (and only one) paper log to use as a firestarter. Both times, we had to rely on icy, wet wood from the woodpile in our yard to keep us warm through the night.

In 1994, our woodpile sat under a large hickory tree. I frantically chopped apart frozen wood while large branches cracked ominously overhead. In 2002, the wood in the pile was rotten. As we carried the black planks into the house, my daughter said wryly, "You know what rots wood: little animals."

Both times, the fire threatened to die with the paper log. In 1994, I had an 8-year-old and a 6-year-old looking to me to care for them. I fell on my face in front of the fireplace, pleading for God to blow on the blaze. In 2002, I wasn't quite as demonstrative, but pled just as hard.

Both nights, the girls slept under blankets on our sleeper couch. I alternately dozed in the recliner, stoked the fire, and peered out the window at the ice sculpture that, the day before, had been just a drab winter yard. In 1994, I awoke at 2:00 A.M. to find the wooden candleholder on the table beside the recliner on fire. In 2002, we used only glass and brass candle-holders.

Those two nights weren't the only times I've felt the stress of grave responsibility, side by side with a deep sense of inability. The girls who used to be 8 and 6 are now teenagers. Ice or no ice, I've spent a lot of time on my face in darkness, crying for God to intervene and, in particular, to keep me from doing something disastrous.

As on those two nights, he hasn't immediately removed the problem or made it easy to handle. But in my weariness, I keep hearing the admonition of a God-spokesman named Isaiah: *Let him who walks in the dark, who has no light, trust in the name of the Lord and rely on his God* (Isa. 50:10 NIV).

Today, those two long nights encourage me. In both cases, we survived. What's more, the power came on and my husband came home the next day. Each night seemed eternal but, in reality, it didn't last long at all.

Snapshot 92

□

Scurvy!

The subject had never come up in our family, that I recall. But that evening, it did. Watching Megan eat her second grilled-cheese supper in three days, I cried, "If you get scurvy, it will be my fault!"

Smiling indulgently, she hugged me. "I won't get scurvy," she said. She's 18, after all. She could have fixed the two of us a balanced meal—except that she had walked in the door just minutes before me, and almost as exhausted from a full day's work.

Still, my guilt lingered, for I am an educated woman. I know the basic food groups. I strongly suspect that the mummies of Egypt still exist because their mothers built their meals around the food pyramid.

And now, since the subject has come up, I've checked into this scurvy thing. It's worse than I thought.

Webster's Revised Unabridged Dictionary describes it this way: "A disease characterized by livid spots, especially about the thighs and legs, due to extravasation [no, that's not a misprint] of blood, and by spongy gums, and bleeding from almost all the mucous membranes. It is accompanied by paleness, languor, depression, and general debility. It is occasioned by confinement, innutritious food, and hard labor, but especially by lack of fresh vegetable food, or confinement for a long time to a limited range of food, which is incapable of repairing the waste of the system."

Alas, I do sometimes fear that I, the working mom, may doom my children to this dreadful disease by serving them "innutritious food." I, who buy whole wheat bread and one-percent milk, have not been faithful lo these many days to serve "fresh vegetable food" at each meal.

And though you sense that I jest, and though my daughters are both old enough to grab a carrot for themselves from the fridge, yet the whisper inside my head continues: "You're not a good mom."

My teenage daughters' salvation may lie in this: Though they sometimes lack veggies, they do not suffer "confinement" and, only rarely, "hard labor."

But though I do, truly, want to feed my family well and though I carry the weight of it when I don't, my scrutiny of scurvy has also brought me another insight. You see, the word *scurvy* can not only be a noun, naming a disease, but also an adjective meaning "low, low-down, miserable, vulgar, mean, contemptible, scummy."

This adjective can be adapted to create such observations as: "He acted scurvily!" "I've never seen such scurviness!" "They are scurvier than most, but she is the scurviest of all!"

In the Old Testament, a priest with scurvy couldn't serve in the holy place. (Don't believe me? Check Leviticus 21:18–20 KJV.) Today, we can't present ourselves before God in behalf of others when our character and behavior is, to him, scummy. Nor can we consistently do what is admirable, honorable, noble, ethical, or respectable apart from consistently partaking the proper food.

As Jesus said, *"Man does not live on bread alone* [else he gets scurvy], *but on every word that comes from the mouth of God"* (*Matt. 4:4 NIV*—my comment in brackets).

Knowing I find God's words, not at the local market, but in the Bible, may I treasure *"the words of His mouth more than my necessary food" (Job 23:12 NASU)*.

And while I'm making every effort to keep broccoli before my family, may I also continually guard against feeding others a diet of innutritious words. Rather, may I offer them ample servings of the words of life. Every day, may I say those things that eradicate scurvy of the soul.

Snapshot 93

□

Runaway Pride

One Thanksgiving weekend, my family and I spent an evening in a motel room watching the movie, *Runaway Bride*. As the movie began, I could identify with the main character's dilemma. A newspaper columnist, he faced a deadline—with no article written and (worse) no idea for an article in sight.

Of course, this character was male, and he wrote for *USA Today* (two things I've never experienced). He also solved his dilemma in a way I hope I would not. Taking the word of a drunken, bitter man (and not bothering to check the facts), he wrote a piece lambasting a woman who had supposedly lured seven or eight men to the wedding altar—and then bolted at the last minute, leaving her husbands-not-to-be single and heartsick.

When the column appeared in print, the woman in question wrote a letter to the editor protesting that the piece contained numerous inaccuracies (for example, she had only left three men at the altar and was soon to try a fourth time). Fearing a lawsuit, the newspaper fired the columnist.

I'm not Paul Harvey, so you'll have to see the movie to learn the rest of the story. But in this very human world (which includes a very human me), I continually run upon a different type of disgusting behavior that deserves lambasting.

In one particular case, I know I've got my facts straight, because I personally witnessed the whole thing. It involved—runaway pride.

A certain man was teaching a class, and he was doing a good job. But smack in the middle of making an important point, he began giving himself a whole lot of ill-disguised pats on the back. He told us things that didn't contribute one bit to our understanding, but apparently were meant to elevate him in our eyes.

For me, his boasts did just the opposite. Yet others in the class didn't seem to notice or mind.

This wasn't the first time I'd sat under this man's teaching, nor the first time his pride had shouted louder at me than the points he was trying to make. Why did his attitude bother me so? Maybe because I too have flirted with runaway pride and thought I would come out the winner.

But like the woman in the movie who kept starting down the aisle only to run, pride always promises happiness and produces emptiness. It leaves the person who tries to wed it devastated.

Proverbs 16:18 says, *"Pride goes before destruction, a haughty spirit before a fall" (NIV)*. That's not just a witty saying, as many of us have learned the hard way. It's a truth none of us can circumvent.

One king with the unlikely name of Uzziah reigned 52 years and did a great job—until the last year. Then everything—his reign, his life—rapidly crumbled. What happened? According to 2 Chronicles 26:16, *"after Uzziah became powerful, his pride led to his downfall" (NIV)*.

An even more powerful king named (get ready) Nebuchadnezzar once ruled the great Babylonian empire. This king had the entire world at his fingertips. *"But when his heart became arrogant and hardened with pride, he was deposed from his royal throne and stripped of his glory" (Dan. 5:20 NIV)*. For a time, the guy literally ate grass.

But unlike Uzziah, Nebuchadnezzar made a comeback because he humbled himself and *"acknowledged that the Most High God is sovereign" (Dan. 5:21 NIV)*. You can read the rest of his fascinating story in Daniel 4–5.

Runaway pride goes way beyond healthy self-esteem. When we embrace it, it will betray us. Only by wedding humility will anyone ever find bliss.

Snapshot 94

□

And the Winner Is Not . . .

"GERALD BRUNT HAS WON $1,000.00 CASH."

The bold white-on-black statement across the top of the page commanded my attention. "Is this real?" I asked Jerry, who had just handed the letter to me. He shrugged. I examined the printed sheet more closely.

Just above the grand announcement, in regular black print, was the qualifier, the IF on which Jerry's winnings hung. "If you respond with the Winning Award Claim Number before the deadline date," it said.

Reading further, I saw other lines that seemed to indicate Jerry did have the winning number: "This is a pre-selected sweepstakes. That means you have already won a cash award."

And, "It's official! Claim Number X, which was entered in your name in the ALL CASH SWEEPSTAKES, is a guaranteed cash award recipient. It's a pleasure to tell you that a check will be issued in your name and rushed to you via USPS as soon as you verify your name and address and your Cash Award Claim Number."

To rake in his winnings, all Jerry had to do was call a certain 900 number. The call would cost $3.98 per minute with the "estimated average call" running three minutes.

I smelled a rat.

One winter day, I smelled a dead mouse in one end of our home. After looking everywhere for it and finally deciding it must have gotten stuck in an air duct under the house, I found it unexpectedly under the sink in our daughters' bathroom. Lured by an undiscerning appetite, the fellow had met his demise in a plastic bag of hair rollers.

Jerry's letter reeked of the same unmistakable odor. Following the smell, I found the sweepstakes rat in the fine print on the back of the letter.

Apparently, one million people had been notified they'd "won $1,000.00." But only one person's number would win that amount. One other number would bring $500.

"All additional respondents with valid ID numbers will receive an equal share of a $3,000.00 bonus pool," the fine print said, adding this reassurance: "in no event will any award be less than $.68."

Just think. We could have made a $12 phone call to claim a cash award of 68 cents. Meanwhile, if even one-fourth of the million "winners" do make that call, T. Hawkins, who signed the letter, could rake in $3 million—and have to give only $4,500 of it away in prize money.

Apparently, Mr. (or Ms.) Hawkins is banking on the truth of 1 Timothy 6:9: *"People who want to get rich fall into temptation and a trap and into many foolish and harmful desires that plunge men into ruin and destruction" (NIV)*.

Ah, but truth applies to T. Hawkins, as much as to the people he is trying to trap. If left unchecked, his own greed will one day plunge him into something akin to a bag of hair rollers.

Snapshot 95

□

Armadillo Road-kill

It was a bad weekend for armadillos—at least, for those living along the highway between Oklahoma City and the Oklahoma panhandle. Every few minutes, my friend and I passed the body of yet another armored critter lying by the roadside.

After the umpteenth body, my friend asked, "Why did the chicken cross the road?"

"I don't know."

"To show the armadillo it could be done."

Callously, we laughed. Previously, I wouldn't have understood the joke. In the other states where I've lived, I don't recall armadillos among the road-kill.

Thus, after an entire weekend of close encounters with little felled soldiers still in their armor, I realized my deplorable ignorance in regard to these creatures. Happily, the Texas Parks & Wildlife website came to my rescue.

Now you can ask me practically anything about "Dasypus novem-cinctus," which we studious types know to be the scientific name of this species.

Otherwise known as the nine-banded armadillo, these fascinating, if mangled, creatures can be found stateside in Oklahoma, Texas, Kansas, Louisiana, and a sprinkling of other states. But originally, they were native to South America.

For you who may never have seen an armadillo, they're "cat-sized, armored, insect-eating" mammals. The "armored" part is what particularly fascinates me. According to the Texas Parks & Wildlife website, the arma-dillo's "bony, scaled shell" protects it from attacks by predators. The web-site also makes this statement, the veracity of which I can verify: "Unfortu-nately, armadillos often fall victim to automobiles and are frequently found dead on roadsides."

Hmm. With profuse thanks to the chicken for trying to set a good example, maybe armadillos need more than encouragement. Maybe they need different equipment. Now that they've migrated from South American wilderness to North American highways, the armor that was an asset has become a liability.

In another era entirely, it was a bad month for the army in which David's brothers fought. Day after day, a giant named Goliath taunted the army, daring any man to fight him, insisting that winner take all. One day, the boy David walked into camp to bring a care package of bread and cheese. Hearing the giant's boasts, David got himself appointed to fight Goliath.

Approaching David, the giant sneered in contempt. He cursed David by the names of his gods. It certainly seemed the lad was about to meet the same fate as an armadillo challenging a Mack truck. Ah, but Goliath was looking at the situation all wrong. For he was the one wearing a heavy *"coat of scale armor" (1 Sam. 17:5 NIV)*—and challenging a Mack truck.

David had been offered armor but had refused it. So did the boy win the battle with a sling and a stone? Yes—and no.

Facing Goliath, David cried, *"This day the Lord will hand you over to me, and I'll strike you down and cut off your head. Today I will give the carcasses of the Philistine army to the birds of the air and the beasts of the earth, and the whole world will know that there is a God in Israel. All those gathered here will know that it is not by sword or spear that the Lord saves; for the battle is the Lord's" (1 Sam. 17:46–47 NIV).*

Like armadillos on an Oklahoma highway, Goliath wore impressive armor—only to become road-kill. You see, a man needs to move quickly to avoid a stone flying from a sling. Goliath's 125-pound armor didn't allow quickness.

So what do you think? Is this the story of cat-sized mammals and a felled giant? Or is it the story of every person who thinks a hard shell and reckless bravado are all that's needed to successfully challenge God?

Snapshot 96

□

Honeysuckle

While the honeysuckle's blooming in Mississippi, could someone please help me get there?

We have a plant here in Oklahoma that looks like honeysuckle. I think people even call it honeysuckle. But I can stand right in front of it, with my nose almost in the blooms, and still get only a hint of fragrance.

In Mississippi, you can smell honeysuckle long before you see it. If even a small vine is blooming, the fragrance pervades the air, rather like the fragrance of the orange blossoms in central Florida during the month of March.

Wait. Let me qualify that. Like orange blossoms, honeysuckle has a pervasive fragrance. To avoid it, you'd have to quit breathing. But anyone who's ever smelled honeysuckle knows it has its own unmistakable aroma, not a March aroma, but a summer's-finally-here aroma.

Just thinking about it, I'm a kid standing barefoot, picking the blossoms and sipping the nectar. I'm a college student on school break, walking the back road to my grandparents' house and inhaling the heady perfume. I'm a mother of preschoolers, watching my daughters discover the extravagant odor wafting from the fence behind our house.

And yet, alas, I'm just thinking about it—not experiencing it. When I do find honeysuckle hereabouts, I'm sorely disappointed. The sight is lovely. But I want to cry, "Where's the scent?"

In Mississippi, honeysuckle not only looks like it's supposed to look. It smells like it's supposed to smell. And therein lies a striking picture for those of us who like to sport the title "Christian."

"Through us, [God] brings knowledge of Christ," says *The Message* version of 2 Corinthians 2. *"Everywhere we go, people breathe in the exquisite fragrance. Because of Christ, we give off a sweet scent . . ." (vv. 14–15).*

So let's say you're not a Christian. What should happen when you find

205

yourself anywhere in the vicinity of people who are? You should encounter an unmistakable fragrance that you'd have to stop breathing to avoid.

This fragrance may repel you—but not because the person it's emanating from is obnoxious. If a Christian is obnoxious or undependable or tight-fisted, sour or bitter or lazy, crude or critical or catty, you're getting a whiff of an odor, all right, but not the aroma I'm talking about. The aroma of a Christian who's gently walking in God-pleasing paths may repel you, but only because it's such a different aroma from what your life exudes. By its very sweetness, this fragrance exposes displeasing smells we otherwise might not acknowledge.

And yet this same aroma will also beckon. Its sweetness will draw you, not so much to a person as to the God that person serves. That's because the aroma comes, not from the person, but from God.

When you encounter someone who overwhelms you with God's fragrance, you may not know whether to run away from the smell or run toward it. I'd recommend running toward it—because when you do, the aroma you're embracing has a way of replacing the stench in your own life that you didn't want to admit was there.

But what if you're up close and personal with a Christian—yet can't get a whiff of the exquisite fragrance I've described? Let me just say that the fault doesn't lie with your nose. No matter how lovely the façade, if those of us who call ourselves Christian don't smell like we're supposed to smell, you have every right to be sorely disappointed. And, hey, I give you permission to come right out and ask, "Where's the scent?"

Quite frankly, if you don't confront us with that question, God will.

Snapshot 97

□

Walks to Remember

The walking started B.C. (before children). In those days, my husband and I lived near the First Presbyterian Church in Corinth, Mississippi. I started walking for exercise but soon progressed to jogging a couple of miles a day, three or four days a week.

Later, we moved to the country, and new challenges arose. First, my knees loudly protested the jogging business. So, I relented and walked.

Second, the blackbird decided to plague me. He'd perch on a telephone wire high above the street and swoop down in attack mode whenever I passed. I took to carrying a big stick—a bird stick, if you will. When he'd come swooping, I'd go to swirling, stick held high.

To add to the fun, I became pregnant. Eight months along, I was still walking, carrying my stick, and trying desperately—but unsuccessfully—to imagine childbirth and motherhood. Knowing it was going to happen, I simply could not grasp it.

After Megan was born, walking changed to doing aerobics with a cassette tape. Picture me making up motions to Christian music based on the verbal directions given. It was—innovative.

When Megan was four months old, we moved to Memphis. There I tried bicycling with her riding behind me in a child seat. On a good day, she enjoyed our biking trip for exactly 11 minutes. After that, she fussed. The afternoon someone started shooting firecrackers near the street where we were riding, she began screaming, and I began sobbing.

Thoroughly traumatized, I gave up biking. Shortly afterward, we moved back to Corinth, just in time for Amanda to be born. Ah, the preschool years! While our daughters played around my feet, I returned to jogging—on a mini-trampoline.

Then came the Indiana era. With both girls in elementary school, I had time again! Two mornings a week, I walked the streets of my neighborhood. A third morning, I walked with my friend Laurie and her toy collie, Marlin. That is, Laurie and I walked. Marlin frolicked.

Those years, this Mississippi girl grew tough. I walked in snow—wearing heavy boots and just short of a ton of clothing. I walked in wind—hurling my body forward against the kind of gales that created horizontal rain and sent plastic swimming pools bounding down the street.

Our move to Oklahoma coincided with the girls' secondary years. Working fulltime for the first time since their births, trying to shuttle teens to all the places they *had* to go, I found again that somewhat regular walking demanded creativity and determination. Week by week, I carved out the time. Hitting the streets, thinking through problems, praying over needs, noticing new details along the same familiar route, I arrived home ready to hear about everyone's day or to put another load in the wash.

Then, our older daughter Megan started college. The evening before she moved into the dorm, I trekked that familiar path and reflected on the places and seasons through which I had walked. I tried desperately—but unsuccessfully—to imagine this new era.

Looking back, I could see patterns and rhythms. Looking ahead, I couldn't see the next step. Yet, I knew I could take it.

In 1 Kings 8, a wise king blessed a whole nation with these words: *"May God, our very own God, continue to be with us. . . . May he keep us centered and devoted to him, following the life path he has cleared, watching the signposts, walking at the pace and rhythms he laid down" (vv. 57–58 MSG).*

What matters here is that I'm walking with God. For then—even if assailed by blackbirds, wind, or shifting seasons—I'm blessed.

Snapshot 98

□

Lucky Guy

Some guys have all the luck.

Take my husband Jerry, for example. He grew up in a large family of car enthusiasts. Every self-respecting family member worked in some way in the auto industry. All were intimately acquainted with their various personal vehicles, having spent countless hours under the hood. The favorite topic of conversation at family reunions, to this day, is gas mileage.

Jerry's dad taught him how to tinker with cars, how to recognize the make, model, and year.

His dad also taught him how to dicker.

Rule #1: Never pay the sticker price for an automobile.

Rule #2: Never set your heart on one particular vehicle. If you do, either you'll pay too much or suffer from a broken heart.

Rule #3 (okay, I taught him this one): If you take your wife along and she's not a seasoned dickerer, make sure she trusts you implicitly, and seat her where the salesperson can't see her face. Inevitably, she will set her heart on a certain vehicle. However, she'll keep quiet and the salesperson won't notice.

With these rules in mind, a poker face and extraordinary stamina, follow this procedure: Find a vehicle you like (not just one that's pretty, mind you, but one that passes thorough mechanical scrutiny). Make a ridiculous offer—but only after doing your homework to know what ridiculous amount is just below an acceptable amount. Remain compassionately understanding yet unmoved by the salesperson's stories of how he needs this very sale to put food into the mouths of his children.

After an appropriate length of time—during which the salesperson makes repeated trips to ask his boss about yet another drop in price which does not meet your offer but comes another step closer—thank the salesperson. Walk away, as he calls after you, "Surely we can come to some kind of deal here. We're only a few hundred dollars apart."

Warning: *You may never hear from that salesperson again.* But also, within the week, he may call you and tell you that his boss has reconsidered and they're willing to let you have the car for the ridiculous price that previously would have sent his family to the poorhouse.

Like I said, some guys have all the luck. Here Jerry is with all this heritage, all this training—and a houseful of women who know nothing about cars. We can't carry on a decent conversation.

Jerry: "What kind of car was it?"

Me: "A red one."

My daughters and I don't keep our vehicles clean. We couldn't successfully dicker for an auto if our lives depended on it. We forget about oil changes. And, well, we let little things slip. One time, Amanda, then a new driver, had a flat tire.

That is, she discovered the tire was flat after she had driven around with a nail in it for so long that the nail head was completely ground off. By that time, of course, she was riding on the rim. Jerry still asks her incredulously, "How could you not have noticed?"

Two days later, Megan, our college-age daughter, dropped by the house. "Daddy, the low coolant light is on in my car. What does that mean?"

"Your coolant is low."

"Okay. So, is that bad?"

"Yes. How long has the light been on?"

"About a week."

Aghast, my husband ran out to the vehicle, fully expecting to find the engine burned up.

Some guys have all the luck. Take Jerry, for example. Day after day, he enjoys the high privilege of doing what 1 Thessalonians 5:14 urges: *"Help the weak, be patient with everyone" (NASU).*

210

Snapshot 99

□

Labyrinth

My dictionary says a labyrinth is a maze. The sign said not.

My dictionary says a labyrinth is "something extremely complex or tortuous in structure." *Tortuous* and *torturous* are vastly different words—though only a letter apart.

One evening I walked the labyrinth, though that morning I didn't know it existed and didn't expect to be anywhere near the hospital where it lies.

That morning, I walked under tall trees at the campground where I'd gone to teach. Still sweaty afterward, I stepped into the cafeteria for breakfast, then dashed to my room to shower and change. After class, I planned to spend the day hiding away, working on several pressing projects.

Dressed and nearly ready to head out the door, I reached for the mascara just as my cell phone rang. I answered. But it was as if my brain had opened the door to an unwelcome visitor and, on seeing the visitor, slammed the door. After the conversation, I was still rejecting what I'd heard. I was still wondering if I'd really heard it.

John, the father of our older daughter's boyfriend, had fallen in his bathroom. The voice in the phone said, " . . . not expected to live." Megan was out of the country on a mission trip. Immediately, I knew I would not spend my day working on projects.

With commitments to unravel, paraphernalia to pack up, and a drive to make, it was 1:00 P.M. before I joined the crowd waiting with the family in ICU. No change in John's condition.

"The doctors aren't giving us any hope," said Megan's boyfriend Logan, "so if he recovers, we'll know God did it."

"He wins either way," said John's wife, Mindy. Even then, she was confident that the same God who worked breathtaking, lifesaving miracles in Bible times can still do so today. She was confident that dying is even better than living for anyone who has come to God through faith in

Christ—not because death is good, but because what's beyond death is far more wonderful than we can imagine.

These family members weren't taking lightly what was happening. They were shocked and grieving. But Mindy said, "There's peace here." She was right.

I stepped outside the hospital shortly before sunset. Near the front doors, under the shadow of the building, I found the Labyrinth Prayer Garden.

"Garden?" I thought, reading the sign. It looked more like a circular tiled patio, surrounded by a single row of bushes, with a cluster of pine trees on the north side. To the east, red begonias and dainty gold flowers grew beside a stone altar, topped with a concrete cross.

On the circular patio, red and white tiles created a pattern similar to a maze—but not. In the center, all-white tiles formed what looked like a large flower with six petals. The sign invited me to walk the path created by the white tiles. I walked and prayed.

The path was definitely *tortuous,* winding back on itself again and again, taking me in a new and often unexpected direction every few steps. But there was nothing *torturous*—nothing cruelly painful—about the walk. Instead, there was peace there.

I did not know then that John would be pronounced dead two days later. I did not know that Megan's boyfriend would soon become her fiancé. But I saw as I walked that no step left me at a dead end. Just as the sign had said, the path led to the center—and out again.

In Psalm 16:11, the poet said to God, *"You reveal the path of life to me" (HCSB).* That poet knew what we are learning: Life without God is a torturous maze; life with him, a labyrinth.

Snapshot 100

❑

Summit

It was 1953, and a first-class stamp cost three cents. In January, General Dwight D. Eisenhower was inaugurated as President; his Vice President, Richard M. Nixon. In March, Soviet dictator Josef Stalin died. Midyear, the Korean War ended.

The New York Yankees defeated the Brooklyn Dodgers to win the World Series for the fifth consecutive time. Earnest Hemingway's *The Old Man and the Sea* won the Pulitzer Prize for fiction.

Ah, but the most popular fiction book was *The Robe,* perhaps because the movie by the same name debuted that year, the first major motion picture filmed in wide-screen CinemaScope. Norman Vincent Peale's *The Power of Positive Thinking* was the second most popular nonfiction book, beaten out only by *The Holy Bible: Revised Standard Version.*

People were singing, "Doggie in the Window," "I Believe," and "Stranger in Paradise." They were watching *Red Skelton, Dragnet*—and Lucy. Yes, it was 1953 when Lucille Ball gave birth to Desi Arnaz, Jr., on the same day the fictional Little Ricky was born on *I Love Lucy.* When the first issue of *TV Guide* hit the newsstands shortly afterward, Lucy and son Desi graced the cover.

And speaking of firsts, open-heart surgery was first successfully performed in Philadelphia. On the other side of the world, Sir Edmund Hillary led the first team to stand atop the summit of Mt. Everest.

But of all the significant things that happened in 1953, my personal favorite took place in West Monroe, Louisiana. A young lawyer claimed the hand of a young musician in marriage. The young man was a veteran of World War II, having enlisted before he was officially old enough. The young woman was a recent college grad who had taken a job playing the piano at his church.

He asked her out. She went. On the third date, he proposed. She said yes. They tied the knot in her hometown. They lived in his.

A tree in the church courtyard caught fire during their wedding ceremony. They said their vows to the background music of sirens. And speaking of chaos, she bore him four children.

They weren't on TV. They didn't write a book. They didn't lead a country or make a major scientific breakthrough. They didn't write a song, unless you count the one he sang to his children on school days: "Oh, how I hate to get up in the morning. Oh, how I hate to get out of bed!"

But today, they're standing on a summit, of sorts. October 17, 2003, marked their 50th wedding anniversary.

In the months prior to that date, record numbers of people made it to the top of the world's tallest mountain. Earlier in the year, a 70-year-old man and a 15-year-old girl successfully made the climb. But even with population growth and longer lives, fewer folks seem to be celebrating half a century of marriage to the same person. In all of life's arenas, fewer practice faithfulness.

Thank you, Doris and Jimmy Price. If it weren't for you, my sisters and brother and I wouldn't be where we are. Actually, we wouldn't be who we are. You've given us life, and you've shown us what it means to be faithful, to each other and to God. Together, you echo the prayer of Psalm 61:8: *"I will ever sing praise to your name and fulfill my vows" (NIV).*

I pray for you—and for all who are braving the rocky heights: May God appoint his love and faithfulness to protect you.

And I wonder: What's it like to stand where the air is rare and the view panoramic?

Snapshot 101

□

Tessa and the Lions' Den

Something has come over our finicky cat. She wants to cuddle.

No, I still can't hold her for more than 12 seconds. But the last couple of days, the feline that usually eats and exits can't seem to get enough of human touch.

The first night, she was lounging on her pillow when I sat down beside her and began stroking her silky fur. She started purring, low and throaty, like a motor on idle. Turning this way and that, she stretched luxuriously, extending first one paw, then another.

I figured our bonding would last roughly a minute. But Tessa didn't want me to stop—ever. Eventually I did, and she left to cat around.

The next night, I was standing at the bathroom sink. She padded over and sat at my feet, looking up at me with an alluring cat look that seemed to say, "So what are you waiting for?" Let me tell you: it's a trick to brush your teeth and wash your face and take off your eye makeup while stroking a cat with one foot. But, again, Tessa didn't want me to stop.

"Who are you and what have you done with our cat?" I asked her.

Standing there, watching her stretch and listening to her motor running, I recalled a story I'd first heard as a kid. It's a true story of a man named Daniel who, as far as I know, had no cats. What Daniel did have was *"an extraordinary spirit"* (Dan. 6:3 HCSB) and a bad habit of praying regularly.

Both got him in trouble. The guys around him, seeing that Daniel was about to get the promotion they all wanted, tried to find a way to discredit him. Unable to dig up even a tiny bit of dirt, they resorted to treachery.

At their urging, the king passed a law declaring (my paraphrase): "No praying to any deity or human except me, the king, for the next 30 days. Offenders will be thrown into the lions' den." Guess who got caught praying?

Now the king *really* liked Daniel. But he couldn't figure out a way to undo the irrevocable law he himself had signed. So, at sundown, he had Daniel thrown into the lions' den. But first the king cried, *"May your God, whom you serve continually, rescue you!" (Dan. 6:16 HCSB).*

After a long night without food or sleep, the king hurried back to the lions' den with another cry: *"Daniel, servant of the living God, has your God whom you serve continually been able to rescue you from the lions?" (Dan. 6:20 HCSB).*

When Daniel actually answered, the king realized: Something had come over his ferocious lions. Specifically, according to Daniel, *"My God sent his angel and shut the lions' mouths" (Dan. 6:22 HCSB).*

I wonder: Did Daniel spend the night stroking those big cats and listening to them purr? Or did he spend the long hours from sunset to dawn sitting in the pitch darkness of that stone-capped den, heart pounding, ears straining to hear a feline footfall, expecting any moment to be pounced upon and eaten?

We might assume the latter. Yet the Bible speaks of Daniel's night as one, not of terror, but of trust: *"So Daniel was taken out of the den, uninjured, for he trusted in his God" (Dan. 6:23 HCSB).*

Facing lions who tore other people apart before they hit the floor of the den, Daniel wasn't quaking in his sandals. He was serene as a woman stroking her cat.

You see, Daniel didn't have lions' den religion. In his darkest hour, he believed in the God he'd served all along.

Snapshot 102

◻

E-mail Response Paralysis

If you're one of the people waiting for me to answer your e-mail, please don't be angry. I can explain.

No, actually, I can't explain. But I think it has something to do with being born in the wrong century. I'd have done well in the days of quill and ink. In that era, while you were blotting, you had time to ponder what to say next.

In today's e-mail e-ra, people expect a reply roughly 4.5 seconds after clicking the *Send* button. That's no problem for some of the guys on my floor at work. They can answer 120 e-mails in just under 12 minutes.

And me? Well, I delete the deletable stuff immediately, especially anything forwarded that says, "If you do not send this warning and/or message of love to your 25 closest friends, you are dirty scum not fit to walk this planet." But when it comes to real messages demanding real answers, I ponder. I deliberate. I labor over the briefest of replies.

In fact, I'm considering changing my e-mail address to copy the license plate I recently saw. It read ALWYSL8. (Ponder it. You'll get it.)

If you wrote me but haven't heard back, I've read your message—and appreciated it greatly. I probably also clicked *Reply,* typed, "Hi!" and, several agonizing minutes later, clicked the button to *Delete* my half-written response. I quit mid-message because: (a) I couldn't think what to say; (b) I couldn't think how to say it; and/or (c) 3,258 other duties, including 71 more unanswered e-mails, were shouting from all directions, "You're taking too long with that one dumb message! Hurry!"

To my brain, the word "hurry" means "shut down." This creates major problems in numerous situations, not the least of which is E-mail Response Paralysis, also known as ERP.

So here I sit, swamped with unanswered messages, trying desperately not to ERP, while my unanswered senders out there in cyberspace echo the sentiment a young upstart named Elihu expressed to a sufferer named Job. With Elihu they cry, *"Behold, I waited for your words, I listened to your reasonings, while you pondered what to say" (Job 32:11 NASU).*

My accusers are right. I'm guilty as charged: a confirmed ponderer. But may I say briefly in my own defense: Pondering may make for slower answers, but it usually makes for better ones.

In Proverbs 5:5–6, a man known for his wisdom uses these words to describe the woman who *"does not ponder the path of life"*: *"Her feet go down to death. . . . Her ways are unstable, she does not know it" (NASU).* Not a good scenario, wouldn't you say?

By contrast, this same wise man declared in Proverbs 15:28: *"The heart of the righteous ponders how to answer" (NASU).*

Now hang with me here. In the original language of the Old Testament, this word *ponder* is *hagah,* a close cousin to our own, "Ah hah!" A man named Vine who wrote a dictionary explaining such words, said, "It seems to be an onomatopoetic term, reflecting the sighing and low sounds one may make while musing."

If we stuff all the meanings of *hagah* into that one sentence from Proverbs, it reads: The heart of the righteous moans, growls, utters, muses, mutters, meditates, devises, plots, speaks.

Notice that the speaking (or in this case e-mail writing) comes after much rather noisy deliberation.

So if you're expecting an e-reply from me, take heart: it will eventually come. Meanwhile, imagine me sitting at my computer moaning, muttering, meditating, musing until that ah hah! moment when I know just what to say.

Sn

□

Heroes

I've decided to become a hero. This was not a casual decision. In fact, the voices around me are still crying, "Fool! Heroes just get trampled in everyone's mad rush to worship celebrities." The voices advise, "Try for celebrity status."

Now that's a tempting thought. As a celebrity, I'd be wildly popular, not to mention rich. Whenever I stepped out of my house, TV cameras would point my direction. Reporters would shove their microphones in my face. I could have three homes and four or five husbands. My life might be anything but virtuous; my thoughts, anything but profound; yet I would be idolized, applauded and widely quoted.

Now—why did I want to be a hero? Oh, yes. Heroes sound a call to virtue and courage. They show the way with their lives.

"Most people don't want virtue and courage," the voices remind me. I recall that the few heroes I do know are often misquoted and belittled, booed and sued.

Take the Pilgrims, for example. They tackled the heroic task of starting life all over in a wild new world. They faced loss, estrangement, disease and death in order to worship the way they understood the Bible to dictate. That all happened in 1620, and they're still getting bad press.

One version of *Microsoft Encarta,* an encyclopedia on computer, describes the Pilgrims as "members of a radical religious movement that broke from the Church of England during the 16th and 17th centuries."

We all know what radicals do: They hijack airplanes, bomb buildings, and terrorize entire nations.

So what did the Pilgrims do to be labeled "radical"? They read their Bibles. Then, they compared what they read with the state church of the day. Something seemed amiss in the church. They reviewed the church's origins. Here's the scoop: King Henry VIII wanted to divorce his first wife (she had failed to produce him a male heir) and marry a new wife (he'd already picked her out). The pope said, "No. That's wrong."

Henry VIII said, "Okay. England won't be Catholic any more. We'll start a new church. I'll be the supreme head. And I say I can divorce any time I choose."

By the time he died, Henry VIII had had six wives. He had divorced two and beheaded two, and one had died in childbirth. The Pilgrims questioned whether a church created by a celebrity of the caliber of King Henry could be on target. Without attacking anyone or bombing anything or even asking anyone else to change churches, the Pilgrims simply started to worship the way they believed was right.

They were severely persecuted. They left England to try to find a place they could serve God in peace. They ventured first to Holland, then to the New World. Life got harder. Death called often. The sea, the wilderness, the winters joined the fight against them. Indeed, the first winter after they landed at Plymouth Rock, they lost nearly half their original number.

Yet those who survived refused to turn back. They found encouragement to persevere in Scriptures such as Isaiah 41:10: *"Fear not, for I am with you, be not dismayed, for I am your God; I will strengthen you, I will help you, I will uphold you with my victorious right hand" (RSV).*

Of course, the Pilgrims weren't perfect. But, regardless what you may hear to the contrary, they *were* heroes. They sounded a call to virtue and courage. And they showed the way with their lives.

Snapshot 104

◻

For a Season

For a season, he was a baby. He grew inside his mother's womb until he lay heavy and low, and she was worn out with the carrying. Just at the due date, she had to make the long journey south, with him kicking and the contractions starting. At last she stood, bone-tired, at the door of the only inn in a faraway town, only to hear the words, "No vacancy."

His mother never said so, but in those days, he was a burden.

Before and since, he's been lifting burdens. Like a mother tending her young, he calms people who are worried or afraid. Like a friend who arrives to sit and listen and cry and hug, he comforts those who are grieving.

He calls to everyone weighed down by financial woes, deep disappointments, or feelings of failure, *"Come to me, all you who are weary and burdened, and I will give you rest" (Matt. 11:28 NIV).*

When anyone confesses, "You are Lord," He lifts the dead weight of sin from their shoulders and hurls it into the depths of the sea. Forever, he is Savior of the world. . . .

For a season, he was a baby. He slept, he cried, he ate. Newborn, he didn't notice the animals who usually fed from his bed. He didn't realize what a toll the trip and the delivery had taken on his mother. He didn't observe the shepherds' wonder or the angels' shout.

He was wholly engrossed in having his own needs met.

Before and since, he's been wholly engrossed in meeting the needs of others. He knows when someone in Romania or Asia or Oklahoma has had a bad day. He sees which families are suffering, rather than celebrating, each holiday season. He knows the exact words you will speak 20 minutes from now, why you will say those words, and what will happen as a result.

He sees it all. And he's always talking to the Father, pleading in behalf of the hurting, puzzled, foolish, wayward children under his eye. Forever, he is living to intercede for us. . . .

For a season, he was a baby. He could not dress himself or feed himself or even hold up his own head, at first. Like any other baby, he had to learn to sit, to stand, to walk, to gurgle, to talk.

His mother couldn't step out of the house without taking him along or calling for someone to watch him. He had to be attended 24 hours a day. He relied on others to nurture him, teach him, protect him, provide for him. At the time, he was helpless.

Before and since, he can do anything. Anything. He can cure the incurable. He can quiet the unconquerable. He can transform the incorrigible. He can provide the impossible and open the impassable.

He can topple rulers, or over-rule them, or use them to accomplish his ends. He can melt the icy hearts of people who've heard his story too often without ever encountering his life. He can get his truth into places where governments and armies, harsh geographical conditions and angry followers of other religions stand against it.

He can end the world. And one day, he will. . . .

For a season, he was a baby. Forever, he is God over all. O come, let us adore him.

222

Snapshot 105

□

Messy New Year

We humans like beginnings and endings to be tidy. Finish one calendar page. Turn to the next.

Ring out an old year. Ring in the new.

Complete one project. Start another.

Because of this propensity, books give us great comfort. They start on page 1. They conclude with the last period. And by the time we turn that final page, all the loose ends have been neatly tied. Movies and TV shows do the same thing in even shorter order.

School semesters, likewise, have a first day and a final day. Between those two bookends, a semester may be frightfully demanding and complicated. But at the appointed time, it's over. Finis. Last semester's teacher doesn't keep giving you assignments or expect you to continue showing up for class.

Ah, but life itself hasn't yet come out in the movie version, no matter what the reality shows may say. And in life, beginnings and endings rarely happen so tidily. In fact, they're usually quite messy and often overlap—like the homework assignments and projects and tests due during a semester.

Funny thing is: We rather expect life to operate in semesters or chapters or some other segments superimposed by people. It doesn't. Life operates in seasons. On the calendar (which people have created), seasons look quite tidy. Each one begins and ends on a certain day. Yet in reality, the transition from fall to winter or winter to spring is far more protracted and far less predictable than the calendar indicates. In reality, the transition between life's seasons is messy too.

Yes, each person operates between the bookends of birth and death. But death is not the tidy ending we may imagine.

And birth? Well, advances in technology have proven what many folks have long insisted: Life is well underway roughly nine months before

223

birth. During those months, the little one to be born receives nurture in the protected environment of the womb. Meanwhile, the entire expectant family operates in that protracted and unpredictable overlap of seasons.

To use a phrase borrowed from a class I took, pregnancy is an "already but not yet" time, when one season is ending while another is being ushered in.

The trick in any time of seasonal shift is not to let the messiness and unpredictability keep you from ending what needs to be ended and starting what needs to be begun. A whole nation with a leader named Moses learned this lesson the hard way. After 400 years of living in Egypt, these folks headed for a land God had promised to give them.

They stopped en route at Mount Horeb for a year's worth of instructions and preparations. Then, according to Moses' account in Deuteronomy, *"The Lord our God spoke to us at Horeb, saying, 'You have stayed long enough at this mountain. Turn and set your journey, and go . . .'" (1:6–7 NASU).*

Well, off they went. But almost immediately, things got messy. When their new beginning didn't prove tidy at all, the people bailed on Moses. Or, actually, they bailed on God. For the next 39 years, they remained stuck—purposeless, powerless, pitiful—until God finally said again, *"You have circled this mountain long enough" (Deut. 2:2 NASU).*

Any year may hold for you a new season. When you find yourself in an "already but not yet" place, remember: Life's beginnings and endings are never tidy. They're messy and unpredictable—and ultimately thrilling. No matter how frightening the change may seem, don't abort the new thing God is seeking to birth.

Trust him. And step into the new season that awaits.

Appendix

Alphabetical Listing of Snapshots

*T*opical Index

Deborah Brunt would love to talk to your group about focused living in a frazzled world. To discuss the possibility of scheduling her or to order more copies of this book, contact her at:

12101 N. MacArthur Blvd. Box 235
Oklahoma City, OK 73162

E-mail: deborah_brunt@sbcglobal.net
Website: www.keytruths.com

TATE PUBLISHING & *Enterprises*

Tate Publishing is commited to excellence in the publishing industry. Our staff of highly trained professionals, including editors, graphic designers, and marketing personnel, work together to produce the very finest books available. The company reflects the philosophy established by the founders, based on Psalms 68:11,

"THE LORD GAVE THE WORD AND GREAT WAS THE COMPANY OF THOSE WHO PUBLISHED IT."

If you would like further information, please call·
1.888.361.9473
or visit our website
www.tatepublishing.com

TATE PUBLISHING & *Enterprises*, LLC
127 E. Trade Center Terrace
Mustang, Oklahoma 73064 USA